Wittgenstein's Form of

Continuum Studies in British Philosophy
Series Editor: James Fieser, University of Tennessee at Martin, USA

Continuum Studies in British Philosophy is a major monograph series from Continuum. The series features first-class scholarly research monographs across the field of British philosophy. Each work makes a major contribution to the field of philosophical research.

Wittgenstein's Form of Life

(To Imagine a Form of Life, I)

David Kishik

continuum

Continuum International Publishing Group

The Tower Building   80 Maiden Lane Suite 704
11 York Road   New York
London SE1 7NX   NY 10038

British Library Cataloguing-in-Publication Data
A catalogue record for this book is available from the British Library.

ISBN: 978-1-4411-7199-3

Library of Congress Cataloguing-in-Publication Data
Kishik, David.
Wittgenstein's form of life/David Kishik.
   p. cm. — (To imagine a form of life, Vol. 1)
   Includes bibliographical references.
ISBN   978-1-4411-7199-3
   1. Wittgenstein, Ludwig, 1889–1951. I. Title.

   B3376.W564K52 2008
   192—dc22

2007050017

Typeset by Newgen Imaging Systems Pvt Ltd, Chennai, India
Printed and bound in Great Britain by Biddles, Norfolk

LeNetta

Sometimes the voice of a philosophical thought is so soft
that the noise of spoken words is enough to drown it
and prevent it from being heard.

~Wittgenstein (Z, §453)

Contents

Acknowledgments

A version of Chapter 3 first appeared in the journal *Philosophia*.

I wish to thank the following: Giorgio Agamben, who saturated my thinking as ink does an inkpad; Agnes Heller, who showed me how to use Wittgenstein as a lens through which my basic intuition about life could concentrate into a burning point; Alice Crary, who gave me invaluable guidance and much needed support on the road to this new yet unapproachable Wittgenstein; Roy Ben Shai, who was so attentive to the language in which my thought found its expression; and Richard Bernstein, who taught me to go the bloody hard way in philosophy.

New York, 2007

List of Abbreviations

Wittgenstein's works are referred by page number, unless the section sign § appears.

BB	*The Blue and Brown Books*
CV	*Culture and Value*
LC	*Lectures and Conversations on Aesthetics, Psychology and Religious Belief*
LWPPI	*Last Writings on the Philosophy of Psychology, Vol. I*
LWPPII	*Last Writings on the Philosophy of Psychology, Vol. II*
NB	*Notebooks 1914–1916*
OC	*On Certainty*
PG	*Philosophical Grammar*
PI	*Philosophical Investigations*
PO	*Philosophical Occasions, 1912–1951*
PR	*Philosophical Remarks*
RC	*Remarks on Color*
RFM	*Remarks on the Foundations of Mathematics*
RPPI	*Remarks on the Philosophy of Psychology, Vol. I*
RPPII	*Remarks on the Philosophy of Psychology, Vol. II*
TLP	*Tractatus Logico-Philosphicus*
WLC	*Wittgenstein's Lectures, Cambridge, 1932–1935*
WSP	*Wittgenstein: Sources and Perspectives*
WVC	*Wittgenstein and the Vienna Circle*
Z	*Zettel*

Introduction: World

In the summer of 1916, Ludwig Wittgenstein, a soldier in the Austrian army, participated in one of the bloodiest battles of the First World War. "Perhaps," he wrote in a letter before the fighting began, "the nearness of death will bring me the light of life" (Monk 1990: 138). This, it seems, was not far from the truth. By tracing the evolution of his philosophy in his notebooks from the same period, one will find a preliminary investigation into the foundations of logic. But in May 1916, as the battle commenced, there is a sudden break in the stream of remarks. When the entries resume, after a month of silence, we encounter something completely different, as if the logician that we knew up to now had transformed into a new person. Wittgenstein begins by asking himself, "What do I know about God and the purpose of life?" (*NB*, 72). Then he continues with a tantalizing series of replies that dominates the rest of the surviving manuscript. These remarks are a unique testament to the philosopher's interest in such subjects as God, faith, will, ethics, asthetics, mysticism, happiness, suicide, death, and, what is most relevant to this investigation, life itself. Although only a small part of these ideas found their place in the closing remarks of *Tractatus Logico-Philosophicus*, the book he completed after the war, the early notebooks remain saturated with a unique philosophy of life.

But there is also something quite familiar about the statements concerning life that Wittgenstein made during the war. First and foremost, let us look more closely at the aforementioned belief that the light of life will show itself through a confrontation with the shadows of death. This idea is hardly original. From Plato's claim that "those who pursue philosophy aright study nothing but dying and being dead," and up to the echo of this formidable formulation in Jacques Derrida's last interview, the dialectical relationship between life and death is a recurrent motif in Western thought.[1]

This observation can be paired with another striking feature of Wittgenstein's early comments about life. Take, for example, the same letter that he wrote before the battle began. This is how it continues: "May God enlighten me. I am a worm, but through God I become man. God be with me. Amen" (Monk 1990: 138). When you connect this exclamation with the basic question he asked himself in the notebooks—What do I know about *God* and the purpose of life— you can get a better grasp of this philosophy of life. It is true that what Wittgenstein understands as "God" is far from being a traditional image of the divine, but it is also clear that his first ideas about life, as they are painted with bold strokes in his war notebooks, are immersed in theology and reflect a commonplace answer to the question that has prevailed for millennia. From Saint Augustine's *Confessions*, where God is understood as "the life of your life," to Leo Tolstoy's *A Confession*, where "to know God and to live comes to one and the same thing," the meaning of life appears to be inseparable from a faith in God (Augustine, *Confessions:* Book 10, §6; Tolstoy 1983: 74). In Wittgenstein's notebooks, this same thread of thought is presented in definitive terms:

> The meaning of life, i.e. the meaning of the world, we can call God . . . To pray is to think about the meaning of life . . . To believe in a God means to understand the question about the meaning of life . . . To believe in God means to see that life has a meaning. (*NB*, 73–4)

If the only testimony to Wittgenstein's philosophy of life were the remarks mentioned above, I could conclude by saying that he has given us a crystallization of the most influential and well-documented solution to the problem of life: a belief in God and a confrontation with death. But there are other comments that, even though they might taste like unripe fruit, can indicate toward the new path that his thought is about to take. First, let me return to this curious relation between death and life. Here you can see that death never plays an active role in Wittgenstein's philosophy. In the *Tractatus*, he summarizes the subject as follows: death is not going to solve the problem of life by making this problem disappear; the fact that we will die one day is not what is problematic about this life; death is also not a different kind of life or the dialectical opposition to life; in death, the world does not change but simply vanishes (*TLP*, §§6.431–6.4312). The only importance of death to Wittgenstein's understanding of life is as follows: "Fear in face of death is the best sign of a false, i.e. a bad, life" (*NB*, 75). For the good life, death is a fear to be conquered, simply because "death is not an event in life: we do not live to experience death" (*TLP*, §6.4311).

But this idea goes beyond Wittgenstein's strictly philosophical writings. As we have seen, it was also a force directing his resolution to enter the battle during the war. A few years beforehand, a day after the death of his father, Wittgenstein writes in a letter to Bertrand Russell, his philosophical godfather: "I did not feel sad for a single moment during the last hours, but most joyful and I think that this death was worth a whole life" (Monk 1990: 72). A few days before the end of his own life, we find Wittgenstein wondering about the fact "that although I know I have not long to live, I never find myself thinking about a 'future life'. All my interest is still on this life and the writing I am still able to do" (*ibid.*: 580). And, of course, there are his very last words, "Tell them I've had a wonderful life," which perfectly illustrate the image of a person who is not filled with the fear of death, yet he is still full with the wonder of living itself (*ibid.*: 579). You could say, then, that Wittgenstein is far from seeing death as the key that will open for him the door to this wonder-full life. Within the immanence of life, death becomes a point without extension. The work of mourning transforms into the labor of life. Philosophy is not about dying and being dead but about living and being alive.[2]

Now, if what is at stake in life is not death, but living itself, then "we could say that the man is fulfilling the purpose of existence who no longer needs to have any purpose except to live" (*NB*, 73). Such a life, Wittgenstein claims boldly, could then stop being problematic—not because one finds a specific answer to the question of life, but because "the solution of the problem of life is to be seen in the disappearance of this problem" (*NB*, 74). What is at stake in one's way of life is living, rather than anything that can be said about this life. This is an attempt to imagine a form of life that is not based on explicit maxims or laws, with only one exception: "It seems one can't say anything more than: Live happily" (*NB*, 78). But there are neither reasons as to why

I should live happily, nor explanations as to what the happy life consists of, nor descriptions of the marks of happiness. The happy life, so it seems, simply shows itself as such.

At the end of his *Tractatus*, Wittgenstein returns to "the solution to the problem of life" by observing that those who found the sense of life are unable to speak about their discovery (*TLP*, §6.521). What, however, is the value of this discovery? Is it a life that prefers to remain silent about the sense of life itself? Should I follow Wittgenstein's decision to abandon his work in philosophy after the completion of the *Tractatus* and simply reach the end of my book here? Could one close the book of life and simply begin to live? This may certainly be a wise step, unless there was another statement that makes it worthwhile to continue. This statement, I believe, encapsulates the seed of a radical shift in our conception of life. Let me continue, then, by way of a short detour, which will help to present this statement in the right light.

Baruch Spinoza's *Ethics* is an attempt to bring the notion of God to its full realization, as the one and only reality, as absolute immanence. It begins with a part "Concerning God" and ends by pursuing an "intellectual love of God." Spinoza's God cannot be affected by any external cause, since nothing can exist beyond its infinity. Nevertheless, by pushing the notion of God to its most extreme manifestation, Spinoza brought about its substitution. God's absolute totality results in the equation of His name with that of nature—*Deus sive Natura*—God or nature (Spinoza 1991: 153). One might say that Spinoza, with his God-intoxication, brought the idea of God *ad nauseam*. By creating a certain kind of excess in the notion of God, and then equalizing it with nature, he replaced the basic concept of the medieval age with the basic concept of modernity. After Spinoza, nature became the center of thought. For the modern mind, everything there is, was, will be, or might be, is a part of this nature.

Spinoza's understanding of nature seems to be intimately related to Wittgenstein's understanding of the world. Wittgenstein's early philosophy manifests the full potentiality of the modern concept of the world. His *Tractatus* is absorbed with this notion: it begins with a definition of the world as "all that is the case" and ends with the possibility to "see the world aright" (*TLP*, §§1, 6.54). The world is the totality of facts. Our task is to try and make pictures of these facts through our propositions, to mirror the world in language, since the picture of this world is "the totality of true thoughts" (*TLP*, §3.01). There are things that you can say and things you cannot say. If you can express your thoughts in language, you can also express them clearly, and so your words are a part of this great mirror of nature. If you cannot speak clearly, your words do not represent anything in the world, you do not make any sense, and thus you ought to remain silent.

As is the case with Spinoza's *Ethics*, where the most important phrase in the book, the phrase that explicitly undermines the medieval rein of God on thought (*Deus sive Natura*) is hidden in the commentaries of the fourth part, what I take to be the most important statement in the *Tractatus* could be easily overlooked. Toward the end of the fifth chapter, we read: "The world and life are one" (*TLP*, §5.621). The world, which is all that is the case, is interchangeable with life. Together with the world, Wittgenstein gives us here an opportunity *to see life as everything that is the case.* To use, or abuse, Spinoza's phrase, one may say, *Natura sive Vita.* In the same way that Spinoza's *Ethics* might mislead you to think that it is a theological composition, Wittgenstein's *Tractatus* can make you believe that it is a book written for the glory of formal logic and empirical science. But Wittgenstein's *Tractatus*, like Spinoza's *Ethics*, also has a transformative quality. It is a common mistake to read these two works as metaphysical systems, while ignoring their ethical point. After this unification of world and life, the *Tractatus* might be seen as sheer mysticism in the eyes of some readers. But this perspective underplays the philosophical rigor that stands behind these conclusions. As I will try to show, the idea that "The world and life are one" is not a divergence from Wittgenstein's line of thought but its full manifestation.[3]

In his war notebooks, Wittgenstein explains his insight that the world and life are one as follows: "Physiological life is of course not 'Life.' And neither is psychological life. Life is the world" (*NB*, 77). This quote shows that by bringing together the world and life, Wittgenstein is not only indicating toward a shift in our most basic concepts, but he is also enabling us to conceive life from a completely new perspective. Life is neither something objective nor something subjective, neither a body nor a soul, neither a thing nor a fact in the world, but the world as such. Life is not a psychological or physiological phenomenon that can be scrutinized and controlled by the appropriate branches of science. Nonetheless, we still tend to see "life as a riddle, life as a problem of knowledge," which must be solved once and for all (Nietzsche 2003: 44). Today, when it seems that life, even more than nature, is standing at the center of thought, when it looks as if the attempt to master nature transformed into a new attempt to master life, it is crucial to remember Wittgenstein's dictum: "We feel that even if *all possible* scientific questions be answered, the problems of life have still not been touched at all" (*TLP*, §6.52). So if we change our habit to read the book of nature, could we really read what was never written in the book of life? But if life is not a scientific concept, could it be reclaimed as a *philosophical* concept?[4]

After the completion of the *Tractatus*, Wittgenstein refrained from doing philosophy for about a decade. But in 1928 he decided to return to Cambridge, where he submitted the by then famous book as his dissertation and dedicated the last two decades of his life in an attempt to articulate his new ideas. In so doing, he was not merely trying to overturn his earlier formulations, since he was also trying to show their full implications, like the implications of the statement that the world and life are one. There is no simple way to account for the differences and similarities between what came to be known as the "early" and "later" Wittgenstein. But one interesting way of looking at this matter is to say that, by coming to terms with his own terms, he shifts the accent of his investigations—from the link between language and the world to the relationship of language and life. Slowly but surely, it becomes more and more apparent that language is always imbedded in our lives. Here language stands; it can do no other. In one of the last entries in his notebook from the early 1950s, Wittgenstein sums this intuition as follows: "Our concepts reflect our life. They stand in the middle of it" (*RC*, 57).

"It is always for living beings that signs exist," he states in a definitive formulation 20 years beforehand. Then he goes on:

Yes, but how is a "living" being defined? It appears that here I am prepared to use its capacity to use a sign language as a defining mark of a living being. And the concept of a living being really has an indeterminacy very similar to that of the concept "language." (*PG*, 192)

Life, exactly like language, cannot be defined, because it remains in a certain zone of indetermination. Nonetheless, by tracing the world of secret affinities between language and life, Wittgenstein is still capable of coping with both of these crucial concepts in a new and unique way. This is in fact a recurring link in his philosophy from the very beginning. As early as 1915, he states that "language is a part of our organism, and no less complicated than it" (*NB*, 48). Could we therefore learn something about our language by attending to our life? Does the understanding of a life rely on the understanding of a language? Maybe this is what Aristotle had in mind when he claimed that man is the living being who has language?[5] This ancient linkage between language and life, I would like to claim, also reverberates throughout Wittgenstein's writings. The search for this living being that we tend to call "man" must, therefore, pass through the demand to understand the "language" that this living being possesses. And this demand informs Wittgenstein's project all along. But his continuous attempt to examine language also goes through a certain development from the early philosophy to the later work. I believe, then, that only after you learn to appreciate the *Tractatus'* meticulous conception of language you could move on to value the vision that Wittgenstein presents in *Philosophical Investigations*, which is the crystallization of his later work. In this way, you may also be able to sketch a new vision of life.

Wittgenstein's philosophy is often seen as therapeutic, releasing the readers from a certain picture of language that held them captive. This philosophy of language, viewed *sub specie vita*, from the perspective of life, is the embodiment of the hope that my book is searching for. In Wittgenstein's *Investigations* it becomes clear that language cannot be simply defined as a mirror of external objects or as a reflection of our inner thoughts. But this is not to say that the words we use aimlessly float in an indeterminate void with no meaning. Language always dwells in the midst of our lives or in what Wittgenstein calls a *form of life*: "The *speaking* of language is part of an activity, or of a form of life" (*PI*, §23). Like the world, language also has elective affinities with life. In the most decisive and the most beautiful formulation of this idea, Wittgenstein writes: "And to imagine a language means to imagine a form of life" (*PI*, §19). Or, if you like, *Lingua sive Vita*. We could therefore raise the following questions: If "the axis of reference for our examination must be rotated" from the "early" to the "later" philosophy, is it possible to treat life as "the fixed point of our real need" (*PI*, §108)? If the *Tractatus* claims that the world and life are one, is it true that the *Investigations* promotes a certain union of language and life? Wittgenstein, after all, states that he is not trying to make us "dig down to the ground" but "to recognize the ground that lies before us as the ground" (*RFM*, 333). Could it be that life is this ground that lies before us? Here, our investigation can begin.

Chapter 1

Form

1.1

I was sitting today on my patio when the neighbors' daughter looked at me from a balcony above. "A Man" she called, pointing at me, "Here is a man!" Her mother said: "Yes, dear, this is a man, but what is his name?" "Man!" her daughter insisted. After some convincing, the girl agreed to ask for my name, and I told her that it is David. She repeated after me, "David," to her mother's approval. But then I wondered to myself: What is the difference between the little girl's two answers? Why does "Man" seem to be problematic and "David" satisfactory?

"Language is the mirror of nature." "Propositions are like pictures of facts in the world." These statements guide many attempts of explaining Wittgenstein's *Tractatus Logico-Philosophicus* to the perplexed. Even though these claims may certainly be helpful, they also tend to hold you captive when you try to comprehend this cryptic book. They make you blind, for example, to the fact that not every word can function like a label that is attached to a thing. Not every word is a simple name. True, the *Tractatus* reserves an important place for such label-words, which Wittgenstein calls "concepts proper" (*TLP*, §4.126). When you encounter an object, like a mailbox, you may certainly use the word "mailbox" while you point at it. This appears like a standard way to teach children the meaning of this word, and the thing that it stands for. Wittgenstein, however, noticed that there are also concepts that cannot be used to denote simple things in this way. For example, in his short discussion of concepts proper, he also indicates that usually you cannot point at the same mailbox and say, "This is an object," as my neighbor explained to her daughter that to point at a man and call, "This is a man" is not enough. For some reason, Wittgenstein insists that this is a misuse of language. "Object," he claims, is a pseudo concept and not a proper one (*TLP*, §4.1272). Is there something in the world that corresponds to the word "object," in the same way that there are things in the world that correspond to the word "mailbox?" To point to a thing and say, "This is an object" is something that only philosophers, like little children, tend to do. Wittgenstein tries to make us see the nonsensicality of these quasi-philosophical claims.

There is, however, still a place for concepts with the same fate as "object." In the *Tractatus,* they are called *formal* concepts (*TLP*, §4.126). Some other examples of formal concepts that Wittgenstein mentions are "number" and "fact," but as you have seen, and as you will see in what follows, "man" may also be considered as a formal concept. In most cases, when we are confronted with a certain fact, a certain number, or a certain man and asked to describe them, we do not say "This is a number," "This is a fact," or "This is a man." There is nothing wrong with these assertions—they are not illegitimately constructed propositions—but they still have no sense, because we have failed to give precise meaning to "number," "fact," or "man" even if we think that we have done so. Which is why these replies would probably lead to the subsequent questions: "Yes, but what *is* this number?" "What is exactly the fact?" or "What is the name of this man?" Hopefully, the answers to such questions will clear up the confusion in the first assertions.

So what is the point about those formal concepts in the first place? When you come to think about it, you cannot define them by means of a proposition or a formula; you cannot say whether they exist or not, and you cannot point to what they stand for. This, however, should not lead you to think that formal concepts refer to some kind of ineffable or mysterious entities. They are simply *variables* that some (especially philosophers) tend to use as if they were predicate nouns, thus confusing formal concepts with concepts proper. A formal concept like "man" could still be used in perfectly sensible propositions like, "A man just fell from the building," since "man" here is a variable, as in "Someone just fell from the building, but I am not sure who it was."[6]

Behind this seemingly trifling semantic discussion about formal concepts lies one of the most decisive ideas of the *Tractatus*—the idea of form. Early on in the book, Wittgenstein states that every object has a form. "The form of an object," he writes, is "the possibility of its occurring in states of affairs" (*TLP*, §2.0141). The emphasis here should be on the word "possibility"—a form is not an object but the *possibility* of an object to partake in certain combinations with other objects that create states of affairs. A certain object can be combined into certain states of affairs but not into every one. In order to illustrate this idea, think about the possibilities of a mailbox. I may say that I am putting an envelope in the mailbox, or that the mailbox is at the corner of the street. But what is the sense of saying that I am putting the mailbox in the envelope or that the mailbox is at Tuesday? This is not to imply that the form or the possibility of an object like a mailbox is somehow fixed either before or after any possible experience. There is no a priori or a posteriori vantage point from which I could know all the things that a mailbox can be or cannot be, this is to say, before or after it occurs in a *particular* state of affairs. Yet it is still clear that "in a state of affairs objects fit into one another like the links of a chain" (*TLP*, §2.03). "Mailbox" and "Tuesday" just don't seem to fit into one another in the same way that "mailbox" and "the corner of the street" do. It makes sense for envelopes to be inside mailboxes, but not the other way around. The determinate way by which things fit into one another is the *structure* of the state of affairs, and "form is," precisely, "the possibility of structure" (*TLP*, §2.033). A form, then, is neither a thing nor a fact. It is not something that exists but the possibilities of existence; it is not what is the case but the possibilities of the case.[7]

Now I will apply Wittgenstein's tactic to the notion of life. First, it seems obvious that if you think about "life" as a concept proper, you will be mistakenly led to believe that there is an object in the world, like a lamppost or a mailbox, which is called life. You would also be tempted to think that it is possible to state what life is or simply point at it. Life, however, is clearly not an object, and the word "life" is certainly not a concept proper. So maybe "life" is not really a concept? Perhaps "life" is only a pseudo-concept? Or is it the case that "life" exists, but you simply cannot speak about it? Before we reach these quick judgments, let us try and think of life not as a thing, but as a complex, or as a fact. A fact is a structure of things and their mutual relations. A fact can be expressed by means of a proposition. But could you seriously take life to be just another fact in the world, like,

"The bench is in the park?" Well, it may be that life is a complicated fact or an intricate structure. But can you really define life as a complex organization or an organism? And if this is the case, can you then think of a proposition (with whatever level of complexity) that could capture this fact of life, since there must be a proposition that could picture any fact in the world?

In what follows, we will see how the solution to these problems will be found in their dissolution, since "life" will be viewed neither as an object nor as a structure. The concept of life, I want to argue, is not a proper concept but a *formal* one. The form of a life will not be understood as a certain thing but as the *possibility* of a life's partaking in states of affairs. "Life" will not be understood as a certain structure but as the *possibility* of certain structures. It will therefore be conceived neither as a totality of things nor as a totality of facts. As a form, life will be perceived as a totality of possibilities. This will be the first step in my attempt to elucidate the concept of life. The central place and unique sense of the notion of form in Wittgenstein's early understanding of language will therefore be an extremely helpful (though somewhat abstruse) tool in the effort to comprehend the notion of life.[8]

1.2

In order to promote the understanding of life as a form, and to avoid the confusions that are imbedded in our endless misconceptions of this decisive concept, I will henceforth use the term *form of life* (a term that will surface only much later in Wittgenstein's thought) as the guiding concept of this investigation as a whole. You will see how life retains its clear meaning only when it is viewed as a form of life. The idea of a life devoid of a form, like the political myth of man in the state of nature, is, indeed, nothing but a myth, but a powerful one nonetheless. I will therefore try to show that life is not a blend of deeds, just as a sentence is not a blend of words. Life is articulate; it has a form. By introducing the notion of form of life, I will try to imagine a life that cannot be separated from its form, a life that its reduction to a simple object, or a mere fact, would simply make no sense.

Now we need to go deeper, down the *Tractatus'* rabbit-hole, by explaining why language, like life, cannot be separated from its form.

This is the force behind Wittgenstein's realization that "a proposition is not a medley of words. (Just as a theme in music is not a medley of notes.) A proposition is articulated" (*TLP*, §3.141). Such a statement can be misread as a simple claim for order and organization. In fact, it shows the very power that enables language to be a mirror of the world. Let me explain. If a proposition wants to be a picture of a fact in the world, then this picture must share something with the reality that it is supposed to depict. Not accidentally, Wittgenstein calls this medium between language and reality the "pictorial *form*." Again, he will explain that this pictorial form is "the *possibility* that things are related to one another in the same way as the elements of the picture" (*TLP*, §2.151, emphasis added). Then he continues by claiming that "what any picture, of whatever form, must have in common with reality, in order to be able to depict it—correctly or incorrectly—in any way at all, is logical form" (*TLP*, §2.18). Think, for example, of the score of a musical piece, the performance of this piece on stage, and the recording of this performance (*TLP*, §4.0141). Each one of the three could be conceived as a picture of the other two, despite the fact that the first consists of notes printed on paper, the second of musicians who play their instruments, and the third of a code that is encrypted by a music player. The *possibility* for such a correspondence, Wittgenstein claims, is nothing but a *form*. The score, the performance, and the recording share this pictorial form. Logical form is the basic form needed in order to achieve such a correspondence between the three. Wittgenstein's *Tractatus* is founded on this ability of our language to be "attached to reality" and to reach "right out to it" (*TLP*, §2.1511). And it is this logical form that language shares with reality that grants the possibility for this rather magical connection. It is exactly because language is *articulated* (*artikuliert*, from the Latin, *articulare*—to divide into joints, utter distinctively) that the mirror mirrors and the picture pictures.

Let us try now to understand better the nature of this mysterious "logical form." Wittgenstein often thinks about this form as a sort of a space. It is, however, not necessarily the three-dimensional space in which we place geometrical objects but something that he calls "logical space." This logical space somehow brings all of our fragmented facts together and makes from them a world (*TLP*, §1.13). When we use language in order to make pictures of those facts, we must present what we take to be the state of affairs not in and for itself but within the context of its logical space (*TLP*, §2.202). Think of the possible movements of a chessman. The rules of movement can be likened to the chessman's logical space. This may also be called the chessman's *form*. For example, a bishop can move in diagonal lines, but it cannot move in straight lines, and it cannot jump above other chess pieces, unless it captures an opponent's piece. In the same way, words also have a certain logical space. To simplify matters quite a bit, I could say that we use the word "Tuesday" when we say "The meeting is on Tuesday" but not in order to say, "The mailbox is on Tuesday." If this logical space is like the bathwater, then objects and words are like the baby. You simply cannot throw out the bathwater and keep the baby in the bath: "Each thing is, as it were, in a space of possible states of affairs. This space I can imagine empty, but I cannot imagine the thing without the space" (*TLP*, §2.013). In the same way that to think about a chessman is to think about its rules of movement in the game of chess, we cannot imagine our words apart from their logical space in language, apart from how we can use them in propositions. In Wittgenstein's logical city, words and propositions, objects and facts, have a certain space of possibilities; otherwise they are meaningless, or senseless, or world-less, or space-less, or homeless. The elements of language never float in a void. They always have a certain *place* in a logical space (*TLP*, §3.42).

Now, if you think of a form of life as such a space, you could then see how a life dwells within its space of possibilities. Again, try to imagine a chessman apart from its rules of movement. Then try to imagine a word apart from its possible uses in our language. And finally, try to imagine your life apart from what you could do, where you could be, how you could be, what you could say, and so on and so forth. Contemplating about a life, one can imagine an empty space of possibilities that are not yet actualized. This is what we call infancy. Henri Bergson explains:

> For life is tendency, and the essence of a tendency is to develop in the form of a sheaf, creating by its very growth divergent directions among which its impetus is divided. This we observe in ourselves, in

the evolution of that special tendency which we call our character. Each of us, glancing back over his history, will find that his child-personality, though indivisible, united in itself diverse persons, which could remain blended just because they were in their nascent state: this indecision, so charged with promise, is one of the greatest charms of childhood. (Bergson 1944: 110)

The question, then, is what happens when we try to imagine a life *without* its space of possibilities? Don't we always need to have a place within this space, a place in which we can live? It appears that one way by which we could imagine a life devoid of any possibilities is to imagine it at the exact moment of death, where the space of possibilities shrinks to a point without extension. But from the viewpoint of a life, the life that we live between infancy and death, the space of possibilities is one way to understand what I call here "form of life." From this perspective, one can see why we always live within a form of life and why a life cannot be separated from its form. You do not give or take a form from a life, because life *is* a form, this is to say, a field of possibilities.[9]

1.3

There are two extreme types of propositions that may be likened to the gatekeepers of our space of possibilities: tautologies and contradictions (*TLP*, §4.46). Although regular propositions (e.g. "The bench is in the park") are sometimes true and sometimes false, a tautology is always true (e.g. "The bench is either in the park or it is not in the park"), and a contradiction is always false (e.g. "The bench is in the park and it is not in the park"). In opposition to genuine propositions that are possibly true and possibility false, tautologies, which are the first limiting case of our space of possibilities, are true for *all* possible situations, while contradictions, which constitute the other limiting case, are true in *no* possible situation. Think about the logical space of possibilities as a blank piece of paper. Uttering a proposition is like an architect sketching a plan for a house on this paper. Looking at this plan, you could imagine what it would be like to live inside this house, where you would place your furniture, and how you would move around from room to room. Uttering a tautology, however, is like an architect leaving the paper completely empty, telling you that everything is permitted, that everything is possible. In other words, this is not a plan for a house at all. Uttering a contradiction, on the other hand, is like an architect filling the whole paper with black ink, telling you that nothing is possible, and nothing is permitted. Again, to call this an architectonic plan would be a bit of a stretch.

In the two limiting cases of tautologies and contradictions we are no longer making a picture of reality. Although a genuine proposition is understood by Wittgenstein as a picture that can correspond to *something* in the world, a tautology is a picture that can correspond to *anything* in the world, and a contradiction is a picture that can correspond to *nothing* whatsoever (*TLP*, §4.462). The truth and falsity of a proposition depends on the situation in reality—whether what it claims to be so is actually so (e.g. whether there is really a bench in the park). The problem with the two extreme cases of tautologies and contradictions is that what is the case can never really matter, because whatever is actually the state of affairs cannot affect the necessity of tautologies or the impossibility of contradictions. You can compare an architectonic plan and an actual building. There is, however, no point in comparing a blank piece of paper or a paper filled with black ink with the reality, because the first may be said to be corresponding to any building, while the second to no building. And so, while "propositions show what they say," Wittgenstein asserts that "tautologies and contradictions show that they say nothing," that "tautologies and contradictions lack sense" (*TLP*, §4.461). As a result, "tautology and contradiction are the limiting cases—indeed the disintegration—of the combinations of signs" (*TLP*, §4.466).

Think now about the symmetric place of necessities and impossibilities in life. Does it make sense to say that within your form of life, within your space of possibilities, something is necessary, no matter what the situation in reality might be, or that something is impossible, independently of what is the actual case in life? It seems that when *everything is possible*, or when *nothing is possible*, we encounter the limiting cases of a form of life. Here we could see how each and every attempt to make such claims (and our tradition is full of them) marks the dissolution of life and the disintegration of its form. At the end of the day, these attempts amount to the same thing: they infringe our space of possibilities by filling it with necessities and impossibilities, by expanding it to infinity or by contracting it to a particle point. As a result, they all tend to lead to a loss of our *attention to life*. Because when everything or nothing is possible, when something is necessary or impossible, our actual life is becoming irrelevant and insignificant. As tautologies and contradictions cannot be affected by the case in the world, we also run here the risk of becoming blind to the actual situation in reality; of no longer being "true to life." In this way, living itself is no longer at stake.

The space inhabited by language and life is neither a space of necessities nor a space of impossibilities but only a space of possibilities. These possibilities become apparent only between the extreme cases of tautologies and contradictions. Notice that Wittgenstein is not claiming that there are all kinds of possibilities but only one that is true and necessary while all others are impossible. Despite the temptation, you should not assume that this is a deterministic view of language. There is no way to bypass the realization that "whatever is possible in logic is also permitted" (*TLP*, §5.473). Even though a space of possibilities is neither a thing nor a fact, it is also not a chimera—it really tolerates different situations, to the extent that everything could be otherwise than the way it is. As a result, "no part of our experience is at the same time a priori. Whatever we see could be other than it is. Whatever we can describe at all could be other than it is. There is no a priori order of things" (*TLP*, §5.634). But this is exactly the reason why, on the ground of these *possibilities*, you must see what is *actually* the case in reality. The *form* of language cannot anticipate the *fact* in the world. The logical form can only show you the different possibilities of a proposition—in what cases it will be true and in what cases it will be false—but not whether this proposition is actually true or false. Even though "there can *never* be surprises in logic," the idea of logic apart from the situation in reality is not unlike a daydream (*TLP*, §6.1251). The logical space may be a space of possibilities, but "reality is as it were an island amidst possibility" (*WVC*, 261). Wittgenstein helps you not to drown in the sea of possibilities by directing you to the land of what is really the case in the world.[10]

Accordingly, when I look at the space that opens up by the form of my life, I see a certain zone of indetermination instead of necessities or impossibilities. Even within a very narrow form of life I still have

virtually endless possibilities. Within this space, life becomes significant once again, because now I need to pay attention to what is
actually the case in reality. And so, in the same way that it is rather
nonsensical to imagine a life apart from its form, you can now see
also the problem in thinking of a form apart from living itself. A
form of life can only show you the possibilities of your existence but
not your actual path. Even if a form of life may inform the way by
which you live, and even if there may be no surprises about this
form, there are certainly surprises about life itself, the actual life
that you end up living. No form can anticipate this life. Everything
you do could also be otherwise than the way it is, simply because
whatever is possible in life is also permitted.

But the reality of our life, like an island amidst possibility, even
though it *could* be otherwise, is actually just the way it is. To have a
space of possibilities without having an actual place in it is like an
endless ocean with no land, like dreaming without awakening, like a
form of life deprived of a life, like childhood without adulthood. This
is the conclusion to Bergson's paragraph that I quoted earlier:

> But these interwoven personalities become incompatible in the
> course of growth, and, as each of us can live but one life, a choice
> must perforce be made. We choose in reality without ceasing;
> without ceasing, also, we abandon many things. The route we
> pursue in time is strewn with the remains of all that we began to be,
> of all that we might have become. (Bergson 1944: 110–1)

1.4

According to the *Tractatus*, the only necessities and impossibilities are
logical or formal necessities and impossibilities (*TLP*, §6.375). But
like tautologies and contradictions, the propositions of logic can give
you no information about reality itself. In its openness, the logical
form may be in force, but it strictly lacks any significance: "All the
propositions of logic say the same thing, to wit nothing" (*TLP*, §5.43).
Whether the world is like this or like that is not something that you
can discover *in* logic itself but only *by means* of logic. The logical form
is therefore not a doctrine that can tell you how the world is or how

it should be. Wittgenstein explains: "Propositions can represent the whole reality, but they cannot represent what they must have in common with reality in order to be able to represent it—logical form" (*TLP*, §4.12). You cannot make a picture of the logical form by speaking about it in language, because the logical form is exactly what allows language to be a picture of reality. If the logical form enables you to make sense, how could you make sense of this form itself? And when you speak about logic, don't you still need to use the very logic that you try to speak about? But it is clear that "the laws of logic cannot in their turn be subjected to the laws of logic" (*TLP*, §6.123). This is the reason why "what finds its reflection in language"—this is to say, its very *form*—"language cannot represent. What expresses *itself* in language, *we* cannot express by means of language" (*TLP*, §4.121). And of course, "What we cannot speak about we must pass over in silence" (*TLP*, §7).

I am inclined to explain this crucial idea by saying the following: *What we are unable to speak about is exactly what gives us the ability to speak. What can be said can only be said in virtue of something that cannot be said. What logic communicates is the possibility of communicability itself. The meaning of silence, the content of this impossibility to speak, is the very form of our speech.* Nevertheless, these formulations must be qualified right away, because they might tempt us to make a fatal mistake. As Cora Diamond and James Conant explain, "What we cannot speak about" is not *something*. The logical form is neither a thing in the world nor a state of affairs in reality. But it is also not a realm that we cannot reach or an object that we cannot touch. As we have seen, "form" is neither a fact nor a thing, but it is precisely the possibility of every fact and every thing. Here you can detect the basic tension within Wittgenstein's *Tractatus*, which invokes, understandably, heated debates and great anguish among scholars. It appears that the form of our language cannot be accounted for by speaking in language but it also cannot lie outside of language, in some ineffable zone that our words have no access to.

What, then, is the sense of placing so much weight on the Wittgensteinian notion of form? Let me return once again to the curious link between language and life. In his "Lecture on Ethics," delivered a decade after the completion of the *Tractatus*, Wittgenstein states that what we can think and speak about are "facts, facts, and facts but no ethics" (*PO*, 40). But in a famous letter to Ludwig von Ficker about the *Tractatus*, Wittgenstein explains that his "work consists of two parts: of the one which is here, and of everything which I have *not* written," insisting that one must read what was never written: "And precisely this second part is the important one. For the Ethical is delimited from within, as it were, by my book" (*WSP*, 94). Now you can see how ethics, which Wittgenstein defines as "the inquiry into the meaning of life, or into what makes life worth living, or into the right way of living," has a secret affinity to logic (*PO*, 38). "Ethics must be a condition of the world, like logic," he states early on (*NB*, 77). If there is anything like ethics or logic, they are considered in the *Tractatus* as "transcendental"—they are the necessary conditions for the possibility to speak and to live (*TLP*, §§6.13, 6.421). And like logic, ethics is not a theory, or a discipline, or a doctrine that one can read about in a textbook and then simply follow it. Which is the reason why if we could say something truly ethical it would be something that everyone ought to follow "with *logical necessity*" (*PO*, 40). This is because logic is to language what ethics is to life—*a form*.

So what is the value of trying to speak about the form of language? And what is the fate of my attempt to speak about the form of life? In the *Tractatus,* Wittgenstein insists that "we cannot say in logic, 'The world has this in it, and this, but not that.' For that would appear to presuppose that we were excluding certain possibilities, and this cannot be the case, since it would require that logic should go beyond the limits of the world; for only in that way could it view those limits from the other side as well" (*TLP*, §5.61). And I would like to insist that it is impossible to say in ethics what is or should be a part of life, and what is not or should not be a part of our lives. We cannot exclude certain possibilities from living. To do so would require from us to think about life while we stand outside of it, separated from its form, as if we were looking at it from above. But this, of course, is plain nonsense. In the same way that "it is obvious that an imagined world, however different it may be from the real one, must have *something*— a form—in common with the real one," I could say that any life that we can imagine must still share a form with the actual life that we live (*TLP*, §2.022). You should therefore try not to give in to the temptation to reduce the form of life to nonsensical propositions, such as, "The meaning of life is so and so," "This and that is the case in life," or "This is how it must be, otherwise we surely could not live" (*NB*, 44).

Facing the problem of speaking about logic and ethics, about the form of our language and the form of our lives, it looks as if the best solution is simply to remain silent. Why, then, should I continue writing? And why should you continue reading? But more importantly, Why did Wittgenstein continue writing? And why do we continue reading him? James Conant believes that Wittgenstein's achievement, like Kierkegaard's, "lies not in the execution of the gesture of pointing beyond the publicly intelligible to something private and unsayable," but rather in that he has "found a way—from within such a condition of impending wordlessness and in the face of such a temptation to point to something beyond—to, nonetheless, *write*" (Conant 1989: 265). But the questions persist: What, precisely, propels Wittgenstein to write and us to read? And why, exactly, do I insist to write, and you to read, about a concept, the concept of life, which has always suffered from the very same temptation to point to something beyond it and faced a quite similar condition of impending wordlessness?

1.5

Perhaps it is the nonsensicality inherent in so many attempts to reduce the form of our language and the form of our life to simplistic formulations that forces me to find a way not to let go of this matter. Keeping silent will be a silent consent with those who insist to speak. What I wish for is that such plain nonsense would be revealed as such. In this light, the *Tractatus* may remind you of the tale about the emperor's new clothes. Saying that what we cannot speak about we must pass over in silence is like pointing at the naked emperor while saying that the emperor is naked. An excellent example for this gesture is the way by which Wittgenstein dismantles in his book the most essential aspects of the linguistic theory of the reigning emperor of logic at the time, his teacher, Bertrand Russell. Although Wittgenstein managed to ground the *Tractatus* on his unique comprehension of the idea of form, Russell was never successful in his attempt to fully understand this elusive concept. One can see how Russell continued to struggle in "What is Logic?," an unpublished essay from 1912, with the effort to explain this concept of form. By rejecting one definition after another as insufficient, he finally reaches a point where the only constructive thing that he can bring himself to say is "A *form* is something" (Russell 1992: 56). But, of course, even this definition is very problematic, because, as you have seen, Wittgenstein's basic idea is that a form is not a *thing* at all. "I can't get on with 'What is Logic?'" Russell confesses in a letter, "the subject is hopelessly difficult, and for the present I am stuck. I feel very much inclined to leave it to Wittgenstein" (*ibid.*: 54).[11]

Despite this impasse Russell continued to develop his own linguistic theory, which was not based on the notion of form but on the idea of sets, types, and classes. Seen only from the perspective of Wittgenstein's *Tractatus*, and simplified here for the sake of brevity, we could say that Russell takes a concept like "object" as a class that contains all the particular objects to be found in the world: benches, mailboxes, lampposts, trees, etc. All the members of a certain class need to have the same property in order to be a part of this class. Think about this property as a membership card that grants entrance to a club. If a thing possesses this specific property, it enters into a relationship with all the other members of the class. We could therefore say, according to Russell, that a mailbox is included in the class of objects. But if something lacks this property of "objecthood" (whatever it may be), it would be excluded from its relationship with other objects and thus from the class of objects as a whole. We could then say, for example, that Tuesday is not an object.

Wittgenstein, on the other hand, claims that "it can be seen that Russell must be wrong, because he had to mention the meaning of signs when establishing the rules for them" (*TLP*, §3.331). Although Russell must give a definition to the sign "object" in order to use it, Wittgenstein maintains that using a proposition in order to define the meaning of "object" is simply a misuse of language. This is because where Russell sees a *class*, like the class of objects, Wittgenstein sees a *form*, or a formal concept (*TLP*, §4.1272). And a form, in opposition to Russell's suggestion, is not *something* that you can point at or define. In this way, Wittgenstein shows how statements like "A mailbox is an object" and "Tuesday is not an object" have no sense, because we have still failed to give meaning to the word "object" in them. These sentences do not really explain anything, because they are in themselves in need of explanation. If a word like "object" has a meaning, it is not because we have imposed this meaning on it, as if from above, through a definition or a formulation ("An object is anything that . . ."), and it is not because we have managed to compose a list of names of various objects ("mailboxes, benches, trees, etc. are all objects"). For Wittgenstein, "only facts can express a sense, a set [*Klasse*] of names cannot" (*TLP*, §3.142).

I fear that there is a very similar inclination to think about living beings as constituting a class, instead of in terms of a form. We seem to be following Russell when we attach a label to a life by classifying it or defining it, instead of following Wittgenstein by trying to attend to the form of a life. In *Mrs. Dalloway*, Clarissa promises that "she would not say of herself, I am this, I am that" (Woolf 1990: 9). Nevertheless, we are still used to define not only ourselves, but also others, by means of propositions such as, "Socrates is a man." But what is the sense of calling Socrates by this name? Are we at all clear about the particular meaning of "man" in this proposition? Wittgenstein states that "only propositions have sense; only in the nexus of a proposition does a name have meaning" (*TLP*, §3.3). A name, I want to say, cannot give meaning to a life when it stands alone. Even a set of names cannot explain a life away. But when you claim, for example, that "Socrates is a man," you might think that you place him within a certain class. You may also tend to believe that you can exclude certain living beings from this class. For example, "This dog is not a man." But in order to know who is included and who is excluded from a certain class, you will further need to propose a definition, such as, "All men have the capacity to use language," which will clarify your work of classification. Such a definition seems to point to a property that all members of the same class must possess. It gives the impression that this property enables you to decide whether a certain living being should be admitted to a certain class, since all that you need to know is whether the living being in question possesses the essential property that defines this class or not, like a bouncer checking identification cards at the entrance to a nightclub.

If, however, you follow Wittgenstein on this important matter, you can now see that the propositions in the above paragraph must be plain nonsense. "Man" is not a sign that designates a class. It is, instead, a formal concept. And such a formal concept is not grounded on a property or an attribute or a common denominator that may be added or taken away from living beings (language, reason, a DNA code, and the like). It is, as we have seen, a sign of possibility. You misunderstand the expression "form of life" if you see it as a method to categorize living beings into different classes. In fact, a formal concept enables you to see a difference *within* the form itself, which demands no definitions and no explanations. It does not matter at all what the properties of two things are, since they can still share the same form and still be different from one another: "If two objects have the same logical form, the only distinction between them, apart from their external properties, is that they are different" (*TLP*, §2.0233). Although we think that we can distinguish between classes by an appeal to their different properties, "it is impossible to distinguish forms from one another by saying that one has this property and another that property" (*TLP*, §4.1241). For example, if you insist on thinking in terms of classes, then you will be tempted to explain why Socrates and Wittgenstein are members of the same class of "philosophers" or why they are members of different classes like "ancient philosophers" and "modern philosophers." If, however, you abandon the attempt to think about their lives in terms of classes, it becomes obvious why, if you see Socrates and Wittgenstein as sharing a form of life, the only distinction between them, apart from their external properties, is simply that they are two different living beings. It also becomes obvious why, if you conceive them as partaking in different forms of life, it is impossible to distinguish these forms from one another by saying that Wittgenstein has this property and Socrates that property.

I want to suggest that the notion of form may enable us to imagine a shared life—a community, if you wish—that is not based on the possession of a certain property or a common denominator and has therefore nothing to do with the participation in a class. We can live together not because we all possess some thing, or some fact, but because we share a space of possibilities. "That I can be someone's friend," Wittgenstein writes in a late manuscript, "rests on the fact that he has the same possibilities as I myself have, or similar ones" (*LWPPII*, 72). You could thus begin to imagine a classless life that is grounded on nothing more, but nothing less, than a form, or a field of possibilities, which can be shared by very different lives. Even though a form of life can never be defined, it still appears to be the adequate medium or the proper mean (which lacks a specific end) that enables us to share our lives with one another.

1.6

Toward the end of his life, Wittgenstein wrote in his notebook the following sentence in quotation marks: "All forms are like and none the same. And so the chorus points to a hidden law" (*LWPPI*, §196). Neither Wittgenstein nor G. H. von Wright, the editor of the posthumous publication, mentions the source of this quotation: Goethe's poem, "*Die Metamorphose der Pflanzen*" (1798) or "The Metamorphosis of Plants." One could wonder why von Wright overlooked this reference, even though he was the closest to Wittgenstein's cultural milieu among his literary executors. This may have to do with the fact that Wittgenstein simply misquotes Goethe's opening. He begins by writing "*Alle Formen*," "All forms," while Goethe writes "*Alle Gestalten*," which may be translated also as "All forms" or as "All shapes." Here is how the poem begins:

Dich verwirret, Geliebte, die tausendfältige Mischung
diese Blumengewühls über den Garten umher;
viele Namen hörest du an, und immer verdränget
mit barbarischem Klang einer den andern im Ohr.
Alle Gestalten sind ähnlich, und keine gleichet der andern;
und so deutet das Chor auf ein geheimes Gesetz,
auf ein heiliges Rätsel. O könnt' ich dir, liebliche Freundin,
überliefern sogleich glücklich das lösende Wort! (Goethe 1964: 147–8)

[You are overwhelmed, my love, by this medley of thousands, this riot of flowers throughout the garden's expanse. Many names you hear, yet each and every one always replaces another with the same barbarous ring in your ear. All shapes are alike, and none is quite like the other; and thus the chorus points to a secret law, to a sacred riddle. How much I wish I could, sweet friend, hand down immediately, happily, the word that unlocks!] (My translation)

Goethe wrote this poem after years of empirical research dedicated to his attempt to discover the *Urpflanze*, the original plant from which all the vegetation in the world came. He was searching, if you like, for some kind of a botanical Garden of Eden. Needless to say, this research failed to discover such a magical plant. Wittgenstein, however, was still fascinated by Goethe's scientific investigations (he also wrote extensively about his fantastic theory of color). The only question is why. Toward the end of the same manuscript in which the Goethe (mis)quote appears, he explains: "A botanist classifies plants. But you don't need a system of classification to show somebody how multiform plants are and how diverse the fine distinctions among them are" (*LWPPI*, §728). What fascinates Wittgenstein is not Goethe's attempt to find the original plant, nor is he interested in the complicated system of botanical classes invented by the poet. He is interested in something else: First, the multiplicity of forms—how it is virtually impossible to find two living beings that are exactly the same. Second, the likeness of forms—how, despite their differences, living beings bear various similarities to one another, which enable us to see a unified form. In other words, *All forms of life are like but none the same.* This is the hidden law to which the chorus points in Goethe's poem, and this is the deep insight that Wittgenstein's philosophy may help us to grasp.

Chapter 2

Picture

2.1

"Ethics, so far as it springs from the desire to say something about the ultimate meaning of life . . . is a document of a tendency in the human mind which I personally cannot help respecting deeply and I would not for my life ridicule it" (*PO*, 44). These are the last words in Wittgenstein's "Lecture on Ethics," which is, up to those closing lines, an attempt to explain to his listeners that to try to speak about ethics is "to run against the boundaries of language," and that "this running against the walls of our cage is perfectly, absolutely hopeless," since any expression of the ethical is, plain and simple, nonsensical (*ibid.*). Why, then, does Wittgenstein still respect those who try to do exactly what he wants to prevent us from doing? Why is it that he "cannot help" but respect the hopeless endeavor to find the ultimate meaning of life? How can you respect someone who desires to do something utterly hopeless? Think about Cervantes' Don Quixote, fighting those giants, who are actually windmills, or trying to conquer a castle, which is actually an inn. Think also about the man from the country in Kafka's fable, "Before the Law." Here we also have an example of a person who is doing something that is perfectly, absolutely hopeless: he spends his whole life standing in front of the open gate of the law, a gate that he will never enter. So why can't we help but respect those characters?

Let me begin to answer this question by shifting back from ethics to logic, so far as the latter springs not from the desire to say something about the ultimate meaning of life but from the related desire to say something about the ultimate meaning of language—to find something in language that will be *the* thing; the thing that *any* proposition *ought* to agree with; the thing that will indicate toward a path, the absolutely right road, which every proposition *must* take, with *logical necessity*. To question Wittgenstein about this desire at the time he wrote the "Lecture on Ethics," a decade after completing the *Tractatus Logico-Philosophicus*, is to raise a very sensitive issue. The attempt to find the ultimate meaning of language, or, more precisely, "to give a description of the proposition of *any* sign language *whatsoever*," might very well be Wittgenstein's shibboleth—it could help us to decide whether we stand in front of what came to be known as the "early Wittgenstein" or the "later Wittgenstein" (*TLP*, §4.5). Of course, there are many stories to be told about the turn in his thought. Here I would only like to focus on "the most general propositional form," this linguistic Holy Grail that is revealed to the reader at the middle of the *Tractatus*. According to Wittgenstein, the general form of all propositions is, quite simply: "This is how things stand" (*ibid.*).

A standard reading of the *Tractatus* would usually lead you at this point to accept without a second thought the following idea as the simple thesis of the book: *No matter what we might try to say in language, as long as we make any sense, we are, in the final analysis, saying something about the state of affairs in the world. Any proposition in language is a picture of the way things stand. The ultimate meaning, the decisive reference, of everything that we say is always facts in reality. This is the general form of our language or any language whatsoever.* But to assume that Wittgenstein actually held such a thesis is to make a basic error that is made by anyone who fails to take seriously the fact that, in both his "early" and "later" work, Wittgenstein explicitly and consistently rejects the idea that his philosophy promotes any theses whatsoever (*PI*, §128). As perplexing as it may sound, he insists that philosophy is simply an *activity*, devoid of doctrines (*TLP*, §4.112). You will therefore look in vain for some theory that the "early" Wittgenstein used to believe in and the "later" Wittgenstein came to reject. Instead, you need to look, alongside the numerous continuities in his thinking, for discontinuities that arise from certain *lacunae* in the thought of the early Wittgenstein, which his later self came to acknowledge. For example, the early Wittgenstein seemed to be blind to the fact that the general propositional form, this form that all propositions in language *must* have, is nothing but a metaphysical insistence. But it was not a thesis; it was like a pair of glasses on his nose through which he viewed language, and it never occurred to him that he could or should take them off.

In what follows I will examine the way by which Wittgenstein came to terms with his desire to say something about the ultimate meaning of language, with the hope that undergoing this process will also help me to cope with my own desire to say something about the ultimate meaning of life. You will see how the attitude of the *Tractatus* can lure one to search for the form that any life ought to have, which is what I would like to call "the general form of life." This is the laying down of the requirement that a life, any life whatsoever, could and should be reduced to a general form. This uni-form of life is something that is essential to life, something that is inseparable from it. Although such a general form may be hidden beneath our various clothes, disguised behind all those multifarious lifestyles of ours, it is only reasonable, one may assume, that we could eventually expose the form of the body itself, salvage it from obscurity, and present it as the ultimate form of every life. Such form, one might hope, will be pure and clear. This general form will be the constitutive aspect of any life; the essence of our accidental existence; something eternal and unchangeable behind the fluidity of our lives; what is universal about our particular lives; the light of truth in a life filled with shadows of error.

"Well," Wittgenstein retorts, "do we have a *single* concept of proposition?" (*PG*, 112). Is there really a general form for *all* the sentences in our language? And what about the general form of life? In order to answer these questions, Wittgenstein requests: "Don't think, but look"—stop for a moment to think about that "general form," and simply look around at all our different ways of speaking and living (*PI*, §66). We then get the sense that "the more narrowly we examine actual language," or actual life, "the sharper becomes the conflict between it and our requirement" (*PI*, §107). So should we continue to try and fulfill this requirement to find a form that will make us realize that our seemingly different sentences and seemingly multiple deeds are actually the same? Alternatively, should we try to show how this general form, which "makes everything look alike," actually hides a "prodigious diversity" (*PI*, 224)? Is there a deep structure, a hidden form, behind the outward appearance, or maybe the form of language and of life simply lies open to view? In conclusion, our investigation reaches a crossroad: should we look for *the* form of life or search for our irreducibly multiple forms of life?

2.2

In the opening remark of *Philosophical Investigations*, Wittgenstein presents "the particular picture of the essence of human language," which he traces back to a passage from Saint Augustine's *Confessions*: "Every word has a meaning. This meaning is correlated with the word. It is the object for which the word stands" (*PI*, §1). Interestingly enough, this particular picture of the essence of human language is not far from the particular picture of the essence of human *life* that Augustine promotes in the same book. A life, like a word, is not understood in and for itself, since it signifies something, it stands for something, which is supposed to give this life its ultimate meaning. Augustine asks: "Is not human life on earth a trial in which there is no respite?" (*Confessions*: Book 10, §28). Life, for Augustine, is like a constant trial in which we try to correspond to a divine thought. In this context, let us remember what inspired Wittgenstein's great discovery in the *Tractatus*. His vision of language as a picture of reality came to him after reading an account of a trial in a magazine. In the trial, an accident was represented by a model of miniature streets, automobiles, trees, and people (Monk 1990: 118). For Wittgenstein, every proposition in language that is neither a tautology nor a contradiction is an attempt to make such a model of reality. For Augustine, every moment of our existence in which we stand our temptations and our miseries can become a model of the real, true, and eternal life. This, I would like to suggest, may be part of the reason for the desire to see not only our language but also our life as a kind of a picture of something other than itself.[12]

Even though the perception of life as a picture may appear to you less obvious than the idea that language is a picture, I think that it is actually quite familiar and deeply ingrained in our tradition. First and foremost, it is based on the claim from Genesis 1:26 that human life is created in "the image and the likeness" of God. This claim, like Aristotle's definition of man as the living being that has language, is a *locus classicus* for any Western understanding of the human being. Curiously, these two definitions seem to have a secret affinity in the *Tractatus*. For example, Wittgenstein writes: "It is obvious that a proposition . . . strikes us as a picture [*Bild*]. In this case the sign is obviously a likeness [*Gleichnis*] of what is signified" (*TLP*, §4.012). And it is exactly these two notions of picture and likeness (*Bild* and *gleich*) that Luther uses in his canonical translation of the crucial passage from the first chapter of Genesis that Wittgenstein was surely familiar with. But to think of life as a picture is not necessarily to see it as a picture of *God*. The seat of this charged concept could also be occupied by a variety of entities that life pretends to stand for. One may conceive life as a reflection of a certain good or a certain truth; as an image of the state or of the law; as a manifestation of some biological fact or a fact in the world; as a mirror of an idea, or an ideology, or an ideal.

Whatever might be your inclination, the crucial point is that you hold on to this requirement that life, like language, should be a model of something external to it. But you should also not forget that thinking of life as a trial, or of language as a picture, is only "a simile that has been absorbed into the forms of our language," which "produces a false appearance, and this disquiets us" (*PI*, §112). This moment of disquietude is the beginning of one of the particularly poignant confessions that saturate the *Investigations*, where you can easily see Wittgenstein battling the metaphysical ghosts from his *Tractatus*. "But *this* isn't how it is!", "Yet *this* is how it has to *be*!"—you hear the exclamations of those who insist on the false appearance that this simile produces (*ibid.*). "I feel," he explains, "as though if only I could fix my gaze absolutely sharply on this fact, get it in focus, I must grasp the essence of the matter" (*PI*, §113). And it is exactly the requirement that propositions should always end up making a claim about how things stand that was the "essence of the matter" in the *Tractatus*—"*This* is how it has to *be*!" Here Wittgenstein explicitly refers to his early notion of the general form of all propositions, "This is how things stand," and he admits that, in itself, it "is the kind of proposition that one repeats to oneself countless times," like a prayer or a mantra, like an obsession or a fixation (*PI*, §114).

Now Wittgenstein arrives at the catharsis of his philosophical confession: "A *picture* held us captive. And we could not get outside it, for it lay in our language and language seemed to repeat it to us inexorably" (*PI*, §115). In other words, the picture that held us captive is that, for language, there is no business like the picture-making business, that language could have no other business besides this one. Notice that Wittgenstein is not concerned here with the question whether this "picture that held us captive" corresponds to reality or not, whether this picture is true or false. He is also not trying to refute this picture, as if it was a false theory. What interests him is to see how this picture *affects* us, what it *does* to us—how it influences *our lives*. It is a queer thing to be held captive by a picture, and not by a guard, or a fence, or a chain. But Wittgenstein knows, from his own experience, the captivating force of saying to oneself, "This is how things stand" or "This is how it has to be!" Because even though the metaphysical insistence that language is a picture of the world is in fact nothing but a metaphor, "now the metaphor tyrannizes us" (*PR*, 82). But what does one need to do in order to be freed from the tyranny of the metaphor of language as a picture of reality, or of life as a trial with no respite? Indeed, by fighting these tyrannizing metaphors, these disquieting similes, these captivating pictures, Wittgenstein's method in the *Investigations* appears to be destructive, as if he is demolishing his early building of thought into a heap of debris. But in fact, the only thing that he claims to destroy is nothing but a *Luftgebäude*—"houses of cards" or a castle made out of thin air (*PI*, §118). In other words, what we destroy is not really a *something*, but a *nothing*—a castle in the air. So you begin by grasping that there *must* be a general form of all propositions, and you end up realizing that there is no *it* that you grasped in the first place. If you insist on fighting against such an air-castle, and this castle tyrannizes you, then you are acting like Don Quixote, trying to conquer a castle that is in fact nothing but a humble inn. You must, therefore, understand that the air-castle is in your heart. For Wittgenstein, to be held captive by such an air-castle is like being a fly that is trapped inside an empty bottle. The aim of the *Investigations* is to show the fly the way out of this mesmerizing bottle, and so to transform us from helpless flies into hopeful human beings.[13] The *Tractatus*, however, is not the bottle but the first step in the philosophical activity that leads to the bottle's dissolution and our liberation.

2.3

Reading the *Tractatus* in isolation while ignoring the rest of Wittgenstein's work can lead one to believe that his early vision of language has no human face. Language, with its particular task and its general form, looks more like an automaton than like a tool in the hands of living beings. The function of propositions is restricted to a single operation—to report the state of affairs in the world, to say that this is how things stand—while other combinations of words are seen as nonsense, and so they are "excluded from language, withdrawn from circulation," as Wittgenstein explains the matter elsewhere (*PI*, §500). This view may leave what I would like to call a "totalitarian aftertaste" in the mouth of the reader. The world, like the state, are considered to be "everything that is the case," while propositions, like citizens, must try to correspond to this totality. If they fail in this attempt, they are not wrong, but nonsensical, or superfluous, and therefore they are "silenced." Everything in language, as in life, is clear. Any question that we can ask can be clearly asked, and it also has a clear answer. Otherwise, the riddle does not exist, and the problem mysteriously "vanishes"—it is no longer an event in the space and time of our lives. In hindsight, Wittgenstein will come to think of this "totalitarian" approach as an ideal that is very hard to shake off: "You can never get outside it; you must always turn back. There is no outside; outside you cannot breathe [since outside there is no *Lebensluft*, no air of life]" (*PI*, §103).[14]

In a lecture presented in 1936, we find Wittgenstein considering the devastating consequences of the insistence on such a metaphysical ideal. He begins by commenting that "people have been tempted to make an ideal language" (*PO*, 358). Shortly after, he offers a striking connection between the ideal language and the ideal life: "There are people today [again, the year is 1936] who say, 'The only real human beings are those that have blonde hair and blue eyes.' It is difficult for many people to escape this notion of *an ideal*" (*ibid.*). This same ideal may also have been on Wittgenstein's mind when he made this uncanny comment in the *Investigations*: "Seeing a living human being as an automaton is analogous to seeing one figure as a limiting case or variant of another; the cross-pieces of a window as a swastika, for example" (*PI*, §420). We can therefore wonder, how can one claim that the only real human beings have blonde hair and blue eyes? How can one come to see a living human being as an automaton? And what might be the consequences of such ideals? Might it lead one to claim that only the "real" human being should live, while the "automaton" does not deserve to live? But in what way is it similar to seeing the cross-pieces of a window as a swastika? Can we imagine "how would a person act who doesn't 'believe' that someone else feels pain?" to which Wittgenstein replies: "We can imagine how. He would treat him as something lifeless, or as many treat those animals that least resemble humans. (Jellyfish, for instance)" (*LWPPI*, §238).

As you can see, this problem is deeply embedded in Wittgenstein's philosophical thought. But it is, also, a personal question that tormented his soul. Already during the First World War he struggled with this feeling of alienation from his fellow soldiers. In an early diary entry we find him counterpoising the human language and the human form of life, in a way that crystallizes our problem: "We tend to take the speech of a Chinese for inarticulate gurgling. Someone who understands Chinese will recognize *language* in what he hears. Similarly I often cannot discern the *humanity* in man" (*CV*, 1). A human life, like a human language, is not a given, because it requires constant recognition. To *see* a human being and to *be* a human being—like hearing meaningful language as well as speaking it—demands continuous work and an elaborate sensibility. Otherwise, if we simply give in to this narrow ideal by which we judge language and life, we are easily led to the exclusion of certain elements of language, as well as certain elements of life.

The attempt to speak about the ideal of language, with its general propositional form, or the ideal of life, with its general form of all lives, brings us sooner or later to a hopeless and dangerous condition in which the ability to speak, or to live, gets close to zero: "We have got on to slippery ice where there is no friction and so in a certain sense the conditions are ideal, but also, just because of that, we are unable to walk. We want to walk: so we need *friction*. Back to the rough ground!" (*PI*, §107). In this context, I believe that Wittgenstein's philosophy is a tool that enables us to see how this ideal makes us blind to the wide scope of language and life. Although the ideal conditions lead to slippery ice, Wittgenstein's work gives us a new ground that enables us to walk again. Whereof a fixation on the totalitarian flair of his early philosophy easily leads us to suffocation, an approach that accounts for his thought as a whole may give us new air to breathe. In the Preface to the *Investigations*, signed in January 1945, the month the Soviet army arrived at the gates of Auschwitz, we find the following sentence: "It is not impossible that it should fall to the lot of this work, in its poverty and in the darkness of this time, to bring light into one brain or another—but, of course, it is not likely." I do not think that the appeal to "this time" is an aside but a key for a deeper understanding of the Wittgensteinian project as a whole. This philosophy, I want to claim, is an attempt to bring light into a certain darkness that is still threatening today not merely the way we treat our language but also the way we treat our lives. In the poverty of the remainder of this chapter, I will try to show how Wittgenstein brings this light about.

2.4

When Wittgenstein returns in the *Investigations* to examine the very idea of a general form of all propositions, it becomes obvious that this ideal is actually a fiction: "We see that what we call "sentence" and "language" has not the formal unity that I imagined" (*PI*, §108). There is no single form of language, no unified logical form, which one can speak of. Instead, the concept "language" multiplies into numerous and interrelated "language-games," as he calls them (*PI*, §7). Different language-games have different rules, and we need not assume that there is a common form that is shared by all of them. Early on in the book, we stand in front of this "great question that lies behind all these considerations" (*PI*, §65). His imaginary interlocutor accuses him: "You take the easy way out . . . you let yourself off the very part of the investigation that once gave you yourself most headache, the part about the *general form of propositions* and of language" (*ibid.*). But Wittgenstein, rather than reprimanding this dissenting voice, accepts it with serenity: "And this is true. Instead of producing something common to all that we call language, I am saying that these phenomena have no one thing in common which makes us use the same word

for all" (*ibid.*). Released from the grip of a general propositional
form, Wittgenstein can now show us that what we do with words could
be much more than just making pictures, much more than simply
claiming that this is how things stand. There is a multiplicity of
language-games, of different linguistic tools, and a variety of ways to
use these tools. Besides making pictures of facts, I can also tell jokes,
give orders, ask questions, request, thank, curse, greet, pray, and so
on and so forth (*PI*, §23). To understand a language, and to use a
language, is not a matter of coming to terms with one thing (something general about language as a whole) but a matter of partaking in
those "tacit conventions on which the understanding of everyday
language depends," which, as he realized already in the *Tractatus*,
"are enormously complicated" (*TLP*, §4.002).

   "The book is full of life," Wittgenstein commented in 1947, "not
like a human being, but like an ant-heap" (*CV*, 62). In his book, *Philosophical Investigations*, which he presents as being "really only an
album," he does not offer the reader a general picture of language
but "a number of sketches of landscapes which were made in the
course of these long and involved journeyings" into the linguistic
terrain (*PI*, Preface). But in order to be able to see this land eye to
eye with Wittgenstein, we will first need to be cured of what he calls
"our craving for generality" (*BB*, 17). You need to realize that in order
to understand a concept, like language or, I would like to claim, life,
there is no need to possess a general form or a general picture of
these concepts. Imagine that you are trying to explain to a person the
image of angels in the history of art. Rather than telling her how they
are depicted throughout the ages, you will be better off simply showing her different paintings of angels. After a few images your student
might claim that all angels have wings, so you will show her a picture
of a wingless angel. Then the student might claim that all angels must
have a halo, or must have clouds around them, so you will find other
images of angels without wings, or clouds, and so on. Although you
lack a prototype picture of an angel, but only different particular
pictures, you still have a good ground to hope that after presenting
all these pictures the student will have a better grasp of the image of
angels in art, even though she might not necessarily be able to say
what her new knowledge consists of.[15]

The origin of Wittgenstein's idea of writing a book of philosophy that is really only an album can be traced back to his "Lecture on Ethics," where he compares his philosophical method with Francis Galton's attempt to superimpose photographs of different Chinese faces in order to create a prototype of the "Chinese features" (*PO*, 38). Instead of giving us a definition of ethics in a single proposition, he offers a series of sentences that, through their "superimposition," could explain to us the nature of ethics, as Galton's pictures were meant to explain to us something about the essence of the Chinese face. But this is more than a careless metaphor. Curiously enough, Wittgenstein actually experimented by himself with Galton's technique in the 1930's. After his death, Wittgenstein's literary executors found a picture that looks at first sight as a portrait of a woman who bears some resemblance to one of the philosopher's sisters. But in fact, it is an image of no one in particular. On closer inspection one can count three pearl necklaces, which appear and disappear behind many layers of garments. The look in the eyes is somewhat muddled. This has to do with the fact that the picture is actually a composite photo Wittgenstein made, by multiple exposures, of four separate portraits: of his three sisters and of himself. By placing the heads of the four siblings in the exact same place in the frame, and then developing those images on a single paper, Ludwig achieved the eerie semblance of a nonexistent member of the Wittgenstein family.[16]

But it also seems that the example of the composite photo is a little bit misleading when it comes to the *Investigations*, because Wittgenstein does not aim to offer us such an *Urbild*, a prototype, or a proto-picture of our various language-games. The problem can be seen clearly when we realize that Galton experimented with his prototype pictures of different races in order to ground his science of eugenics. But unlike Galton's attempt to find *the general picture of a form of life*, Wittgenstein never asks us to "superimpose" all our uses of language in order to create a proto-picture of language as a whole. Instead, he asks us to see its irreducible multiplicity. His methodology is based on this ability to understand concepts like "language" and, I am here to suggest, "life," without giving us a general picture of what these concepts stand for. Language, like life, form "a complicated network of similarities overlapping and criss-crossing" (*PI*, §66). They consist of a multiplicity of phenomena that relate to each other in much the same way that different family members have an affinity to each other, even though there needs to be no single property that they all share with one another. This is what Wittgenstein calls "family resemblance" (*PI*, §67). It is like, he explains in the same remark, a thread that is created by spinning a multiplicity of fibers that overlap with each other. The strength of this thread is not affected by the fact that there is no single fiber that runs through its whole length. From this perspective, our understanding of language and of life does not diminish but actually becomes stronger as a consequence of our awareness to the multiplicity of language-games and forms of life. In this way, we can now begin to imagine how living beings could form communities whose members are singular beings, as the only thing that they have in common is a sort of family resemblance, which is a complicated network of similarities overlapping and criss-crossing. Because life, like language, "is variously rooted; it has roots, not a single root" (*Z*, §656). Thus, the book of life is really only an album.

"How many kinds of sentences are there? Say assertion, question, and command?" To this question Wittgenstein replies: "There are *countless* kinds . . . And this multiplicity is not something fixed, given once and for all; but new types of language, new language-games, as we may say, come into existence, and others become obsolete and get forgotten" (*PI*, §23). Now I can also pose the direct question that stands at the background of this investigation: How many kinds of forms of life are there? Aristotle claims that there are three: the life of pleasure, political life, and the contemplative life (*The Nicomachean Ethics*: 1095b 17). Or maybe, inspired by the young Wittgenstein, we should say that there is in fact only one general form of life. But if we are cured from the "craving for generality," we could begin to witness the countless forms that are woven into our lives. Nevertheless, we should also never forget the "hidden law" that we discovered at the end of Chapter 1: all forms of life are akin and none is quite like the other, just as all our language-games are alike but none could be said to be the same. Despite the lack of a single thing that can connect all our different lives to each other, although we release ourselves from the requirement to find a general form, there is still a whole network of resemblances that enables us to see connections between different lives and to trace not only their staggering multiplicity but also their subtle unity. And so we find ourselves speaking not only about different forms of life but also about *the* form of life, which is what we sometimes call "humanity," precisely as Wittgenstein speaks not only about different language-games but also about *the* language-game, that is, our human language (*PI*, §7). But what prevents us from speaking about *the* form of life as encompassing other living beings, like a part or the whole of the animal kingdom, or even plants?

In order to clarify this idea, it will be helpful to think in this respect about a book that is "really only an album," but not in a metaphorical sense, as the *Investigations* is presented to the reader. I am thinking about an actual notebook that served as Wittgenstein's personal photo album. In one of its pages there is a series of snapshots glued onto the lined paper one next to the other without any apparent order. Some pictures show certain persons next to a dinner table, in others people are photographed outside on a porch, while others portray the subjects next to a grand staircase (Nedo and Ranchetti 1983: 293). Wittgenstein took all these photos during a vacation at his family's estate. When I saw these pictures for the first time, I said to myself: "Don't think, but look." It is clear that all these individuals are alike, but also that none are the same. There is no single feature that they all share, though they have various properties that helped me realize that they are somehow related to one another. But instead of superimposing these pictures one on top of the other, they are simply placed one next to the other. I think that this is an excellent example for family resemblance. It is also a good example of the way photography enables us not only to see how things which look different are really the same but also how "things which look the same are really different," which was such an important matter for Wittgenstein that he contemplated using a quotation from King Lear, "I'll teach you differences," as the epigraph for his book (Drury 1981: 171). In a decisive way, the art of photography teaches us differences—between different lives, and even the differences in the same living being over time, from one picture to the other. Yet, of course, it is only on the background of some kind of (family) resemblance that a difference could show itself as such. One of my favorite photographers, Diane Arbus, was particularly attuned to this task.

Think, for example, about her iconic portrait of the "identical twins" (Arbus 2003: 265). The two young girls stand next to each other with their hands to the side of their bodies. They are dressed in identical black dresses, and their hair is tied in the same way with two white ribbons. But as one girl slightly smiles, the other has a rather serious look on her face. Even though the twins are identical, they are evermore different. The almost paranormal force of this image arises from this irreconcilable tension. In 1939, when Arbus was 16-years-old, she wrote an essay for school about Plato, the philosopher who taught us that the differences between humans are merely the shadows of an eternal and unchanging form or *idea*.[17] Arbus' reaction to this suggestion perfectly articulates what will become her life project, as well as Wittgenstein's own:

> There are and have been and will be an infinite number of things on earth. Individuals all different, all wanting different things, all knowing different things, all loving different things, all looking different. Everything that has been on earth has been different from any other thing. That is what I love: the differentness, the uniqueness of all things, and the importance of life. (*ibid.*: 70)

If a picture held us captive, then only another picture could set us free.

2.5

One can expect that the later Wittgenstein would finally cure us from the hopeless practice of running against the limits of language. But in the *Investigations* you will actually find him going back to this practice and even describing it as a formative experience:

> The results of philosophy are the uncovering of one or another piece of plain nonsense and of bumps that the understanding has got by running its head up against the limits of language. These bumps make us see the value of the discovery. (*PI*, §119)

Now, I believe, we can finally return to the question with which we began concerning the respect that Wittgenstein cannot help but have for those who participate in such hopeless endeavors. We need to come to terms with the practice of those people who, in their hopelessness, with all the bruises that their understanding has got, "make us see the value of the discovery." But what, exactly, do they discover, and what, precisely, are those pieces of plain nonsense that they uncover?

I already mentioned Cora Diamond and James Conant's approach to the silence at the end of the *Tractatus*. Interestingly enough, these two scholars see the attempt to run against the limits of language not as a sign of courage but as a sign of weakness. Diamond even claims that those who try to do so are "chickening out" (Diamond 1991: 181). To "chicken out" is to perceive a pregnant silence that is pointing to ineffable and sacred truth. Trying to speak about what we need to be silent about, trying to cross impassable border, should not earn our respect but our admonition. But should one ridicule these hopeless attempts? In order to answer this question, let us take a closer look at what Diamond calls "chickening out" by comparing it to a manuscript Wittgenstein composed in the early 1930s. Here he describes people who insist on something—like the insistence on the general form of propositions—even though they are deeply troubled by this thing that they insist on. Then he adds, in handwriting at the margins of the page, "Hen and chalk-line," without explanation (*PO*, 175). Most likely, he is referring here to a curious phenomenon: if you take a piece of chalk and draw with it a simple line in front of a hen, the bird will refuse to cross this harmless mark. Even though not only hens, but also chickens, suffer from the same predicament, I suggest distinguishing the condition in which one is unwilling to go beyond an imaginary border by calling it "henning out." Thus, according to Conant, "the value of the discovery" in reading Wittgenstein's *Tractatus* is not the discovery of the impenetrable limits of language but the experience of how these imposing limits melt into air: "In the end the limits vanish—that is, the idea that there are limits here confining one is the central idea that one needs to learn how to throw away" (Conant 1989: 254).

I think that we could better understand Diamond and Conant's approach to Wittgenstein's philosophy if we compare it with Gerschom Scholem and Walter Benjamin's approach to Kafka's literature.

What does it mean, the two scholars ask themselves, to stand in front of the gate of law? Why is it that the man from the country never even *tries* to enter this gate, even though it remains open throughout his life? According to Scholem, Kafka's law can be summarized by the expression "being in force without significance"—the law rules our lives without saying anything meaningful (Scholem 1992: 142). If you like, it is a *Gesetz*, a law, without being a *Satz*, a significant proposition. On the ground of Chapter 1, we can now see how this Kafkaesque law is congruent with the Wittgensteinian approach to logic—as something that is in force in our language, as a sort of a law of every meaningful proposition, even though it is impossible to use significant propositions in order to express this logical form. It appears that Wittgenstein's logic, like Kafka's law, cannot be spoken of, even though they remain in full force over our language and our lives.[18] Nevertheless, Benjamin's position, in opposition to Scholem's analysis, is that "being in force without significance" is a situation akin to that of a student who reads the Scripture—this is to say, the law—but has lost the keys that could encrypt the text and make sense out of it. For Benjamin, Scripture without its keys is "not Scripture but life. Life as it is lived in the village at the foot of the hill on which the castle is built" (*ibid.*: 135). The castle, another one of Kafka's metaphors for the impenetrability of the law, loses here not only its significance but also its very force. Benjamin points toward the possibility that this imposing castle is nothing but *Luftgebäude*, a building made out of thin air, as Wittgenstein calls it, or just a humble inn, as Sancho Panza knew all along.

I need to be a little clearer about what is at stake here by returning to Wittgenstein's comportment toward logic in the *Tractatus*. What does it mean to do what the author is doing in his book, in his hopeless attempt to run against the limits of language? Why can't we help respecting Wittgenstein, even though he admits that the propositions of his book are utterly nonsensical (*TLP*, §6.54)? I think that one answer is that the *Tractatus'* success lies to a great extent in its failure. Imagine that Wittgenstein succeeded in speaking about the logical form, and the man from the country succeeded in entering the gate of law, so we were left with the ultimate meaning of language and the ultimate meaning of life. Imagine that Don Quixote managed at the end to actually kill the giants and conquer the castle. To put it differently, the nonsense inherent in what Wittgenstein is trying to do does not point to a hidden essence, since its nonsensicality is its very essence. Like Cervantes and Kafka's fictions, his propositions are meant to point to the very fact that they are fictions. A few days before his death, Wittgenstein writes: "Am I not getting closer and closer to saying that in the end logic cannot be described? You must look at the practice of language, then you will see it" (*OC*, §501). Instead of looking for an ideal language, you need to see the everyday language that is weaved into the fabric of your ordinary life. Rather than searching for a single logical form, try to attend to a multiplicity of forms of life. You will then observe the life that is lived at the foot of the hill on which the air-castle of logic stands.

2.6

In the beginning of the second part of the *Investigations*, Wittgenstein poses the following question: "One can imagine an animal angry, frightened, unhappy, happy, startled. But hopeful? And why not?" (*PI*, 174). I can imagine that my friend is hoping to see me next week. But can I imagine that my dog is *hoping* today to see me tomorrow or the day after tomorrow? And why not? A possible answer, Wittgenstein suggests, has to do with the possession of language. In the same way that, as we have seen, those who run against the limits of language—whereof one *cannot* speak—are doing something absolutely hopeless, those who *can* speak, the living beings that *have* language, are also the living beings who happen to possess this thing that we call hope: "Can only those hope who can talk? Only those who have mastered the use of language. That is to say, the phenomena of hope are modes of this complicated form of life" (*ibid.*).

We may better understand this beautiful yet cryptic remark if we think about what happens when we separate a mature human being from this complicated form of life, when we reduce one's existence to a limited language-game, or deprive a human being from the capacity to use language altogether. Is it correct to say that if we do so, we are left with a creature deprived of any trace of hope? You can get a rough picture of such a hopeless condition if you think about the life

of the two builders from the beginning of the *Investigations*, whose
language consists of only four words (*block, pillar, slab,* and *beam*),
which the first builder uses in order to call for a building material
that his assistant searches for and then hands to him (*PI*, §2). A question can be raised: Will it make any difference if the first builder *hoped*
that his assistant would pass him the right building material, or that
the assistant *hoped* that the first builder would ask for a certain building material? Do we need to assume that hope is a part of their
primitive language-game, their *un*complicated form of life, or their
poor world? Moreover, one can wonder whether Wittgenstein depicts
here something that can really be considered as a complete language
or a complete form of life?

   These, however, are not only hypothetical questions. As the liar
paradox teaches us something about the question of truth, the paradox inherent in Wittgenstein's builders can help us to cope with
the question of language and life. We can comprehend what is at
stake here if we realize that those builders are not only a fruit of
Wittgenstein's imagination. At the very same time that he was writing
the *Investigations*, human beings were actually being separated from
this complicated human form of life. It got to a point in which some
of them, in the most extreme conditions in the concentration camps,
were reduced to nothing more than such builders, while others
completely lost their ability to speak, to say "yes" to food, and "no" to
pain. Again, we wonder: If these living beings can no longer talk, can
they still hope? This question, however, does not emerge from a metaphysical insistence about the link between the possession of language
and the possession of hope or a metaphysical insistence about the
essential difference between man and animal. It is, rather, an ethical
insistence. By bearing witness to this threshold of humanity, to "the
darkness of this time," the potentiality of Wittgenstein's philosophy
becomes not only apparent but also urgent. It is simply as follows: "to
imagine a language means to imagine a form of life" (*PI*, §19). If we
imagine a language that consists of nothing but orders and their
obedience, or nothing but reports about states of affairs, then we
imagine a life in the camp. But if we imagine the countless language-
games that Wittgenstein entices us to imagine in his *Investigations*,
then we imagine a life in the city. "Our language," he writes there,

can be seen as an ancient city: a maze of little streets and squares, of old and new houses, and of houses with additions from various periods; and this surrounded by a multitude of new boroughs with straight regular streets and uniform houses. (*PI*, §18)

And so, "bit by bit," by inhabiting the city of language, "daily life becomes such that there is a place for hope in it" (*Z*, §469).

Chapter 3

Meaning

3.1

Toward the end of the *Tractatus Logico-Philosophicus*, Wittgenstein distinguishes between two aspects of the world: *how* the world is and *that* it is. We can talk in language about the *how*, but *that* it exists is not something that we can speak about. That *there is* a world is what he calls "the mystical" (*TLP*, §6.44). But in 1929, about a decade after the completion of his book, Wittgenstein returns in his "Lecture on Ethics" to this wonder that there is something rather than nothing. Now, he decides to elaborate on his earlier idea by saying that the expression of the wonder at the existence of the world is *the very existence of language*: "The right expression in language for the miracle of the existence of the world, though it is not any proposition *in* language, is the existence of language itself" (*PO*, 43–4). That *there is* language is the proper manifestation for the fact that *there is* a world.

The sense of this curious remark and its relevance to our investigation seems obscured at first sight. Let me try then to complicate things a little in order to untangle them shortly after. We first asked, "What is the correct expression for the wonder at the existence of the world?" Now, even if we accept the answer given to us by Wittgenstein, the subsequent question must arise: "If the most appropriate expression of wonderment at the existence of the world is the existence of language, what then is the correct expression for the existence of language?" Giorgio Agamben, who raises this issue in a rare reference to Wittgenstein's work, replies: "The only possible answer to this question is: human life, as *ethos*, as ethical way" (Agamben 1993: 9–10).

Agamben's answer is far from being accidental, since it stands in complete accord with various comments made by Wittgenstein around the time he wrote his "Lecture on Ethics." See, for example, the following statement from a text dated from the same period. Here Wittgenstein confronts again the wonder at the existence of the world, only that now the concept of life enters the considerations, as it does in Agamben's analysis:

> What is self-evident, *life*, is supposed to be something accidental, unimportant; by contrast something that normally I never worry my head about is what is real! I.e., what one neither can nor wants to go beyond would not be the world. Again and again there is the attempt to define the world in language, and to display it—but that doesn't work. The self-evidence of the world is expressed in the very fact that language means only it, and can only mean it. (*PO*, 193)

A few years later, Wittgenstein returns to this conceptual trinity of language, world, and life. In the middle of a series of notes for his lectures on private experience and sense data from the mid-1930s, he breaks his stream of thought and exclaims: "But aren't you neglecting something—the experience or whatever you might call it? Almost *the world* behind the mere words?" (*PO*, 255). The nature of this negligence, of "that which goes without saying," as he further puts it, becomes clear when he suggests: "It seems that I neglect life. But not life physiologically understood but life as consciousness. And consciousness not physiologically understood, or understood from the outside, but consciousness as the very essence of experience, the appearance of the world, the world" (*ibid.*). This last point triggers once again the problem of the expression of the world's existence: "If I had to add the world to my language it would have to be one sign for the whole of language" (*ibid.*).

Life, Wittgenstein claims, seems to be accidental and unimportant, since it is always self-evident and open to view. As a result, we tend to neglect it. But now we are asked to see that this life, which "goes without saying," is what is really important. He therefore insinuates that "what one neither can nor wants to go beyond would not be the world" but life itself. Of course, this intuition should not surprise us if we recall that in the *Tractatus* he already makes the sweeping claim that "the world and life are one" (*TLP*, §5.621). It is also important to note that this statement is a direct consequence of the realization that "the world is *my* world," which "is manifested in the fact that the limits of the language (*the* language which I understand) mean the limits of *my* world" (*TLP*, §5.62). This move may explain why the only expression for the existence of language, though it is nothing that can be said *in* language, is the very existence of life itself. Or, as he puts it in *Philosophical Investigations*, "to imagine a language means to imagine a form of life" (*PI*, §19). As I was indicating beforehand, it appears that one way of explaining the development in Wittgenstein's philosophy is to say that instead of trying to account for the way language corresponds to the world, he began to investigate the way by which "the *speaking* of language is a part of an activity, or of a form of life" (*PI*, §23). Even though this basic intuition, which flashes up in the text only for an instant, is never explicitly developed in the *Investigations*, it seems to illuminate much of Wittgenstein's later thought. See, for example, the following remark, which appears in yet another text from the early 1930s: "Well, language does connect up with my own life. And what is called 'language' is something made up of heterogonous elements and the way it meshes with life is infinitely various" (*PG*, 66). Wittgenstein will return on numerous occasions to this life behind the mere words. Time and again he treats concepts as having a "home in our life," as being "embedded in life," or as "patterns in the weave of life," claiming that words have meaning only in "the flux of life," "the bustle of life," or "the stream of life."[19]

3.2

In the opening scene of the *Blue Book*, which Wittgenstein dictated in the early 1930s, he asks us to imagine a person who is mercilessly reiterating such questions as, "What is the meaning of a word?" or simply, "What is meaning?" He then describes this human condition as some sort of a "mental cramp" in which "we feel that we can't point to anything in reply to [these questions] and yet ought to point to something" (*BB*, 1). In a related passage from the *Investigations*, this mental cramp seems to produce the feeling that "*the essence is hidden from us*," which then leads to questions such as "What is a proposition?" "What is language?" and to the search for answers that will "be given once and for all; and independently of any future experience" (*PI*, §92). I would now like to suggest that it is exactly the blindness to the way by which language meshes with life that causes this mental cramp. In order to clarify my idea, I will examine such a helpless condition of relentless questioning, where the essence seems to be hidden. But instead of the problem, "What is the meaning of a word?" or "What is language?" in this example we find Leo Tolstoy asking, "What is the meaning of life?"

> And so I lived. But five years ago something very strange began to happen to me. At first I began having moments of bewilderment, when my life would come to a halt, as if I did not know how to live or what to do . . . Whenever my life came to a halt, the questions would arise: Why? And what next? . . . I could breathe, eat, drink, and sleep; indeed, I could not help but breathe, eat, drink, and sleep. But there was no life in me . . . I did not even want to discover truth anymore because I had guessed what it was. The truth was that life is meaningless. (Tolstoy 1983: 26–8)[20]

"A confession," Wittgenstein wrote in his notebook, "has to be a part of your new life" (*CV*, 18). If the quote from Saint Augustine's *Confessions* that opens Wittgenstein's *Investigations* is presented as a particular picture of the essence of human language, then the above quote from Tolstoy's *A Confession* may help us to better understand what I take to be a particular picture of the essence of human life which still holds us captive. It is as follows: life has a certain meaning; this meaning correlates to a life; it is this meaning for which and according to which we need to live. Notice, however, that Tolstoy does not speak of there being any difference between lives. Since the essence of life is hidden from him, he tries to find an answer that could "be given once and for all; and independently of any future experience." The absence of such an answer leads him to assert "the truth"—that life is meaningless, worthless, aimless, empty, a vanity fair.

Think for a moment about the sentence "Life is meaningless" as a picture, in the same way by which Wittgenstein used to think about propositions during the time he wrote the *Tractatus*. Life is meaningless—*this is how things stand.* A question that the later Wittgenstein seems to be posing to his early self will help us understand my attitude toward such an idea: "The picture is *there*; and I do not dispute its *correctness*. But *what* is its application?" (*PI*, §424). In the same way, I do not dispute Tolstoy's claim that life is meaningless; I am not claiming that the picture of life that he presents to us is correct or incorrect, and I am not asking whether this is indeed how things stand. Wittgenstein, however, still insists that the *application* of such a proposition must be closely examined. Tolstoy, after all, does describe a life, quite beautifully, in fact. But not everything that we call "life" corresponds to this picture.[21] By itself, the claim that "life is meaningless" simply surrounds the different lives that we see around us "with a haze which makes clear vision impossible."[22] But let us not forget that the claim that "life is meaningless" is taken from a confession—it is an account of a person's *life*. Only within the context of Tolstoy's life, as it is depicted in his book, can one begin to understand the meaning, and the application, of his statement. From this perspective, "life is meaningless" may be understood neither as a philosophical claim nor as a report about a state of affairs, but the statement may still be understood as a description of a mood, like, "I am anxious," or a call for help, like, "I am in pain."

But how does this hopeless condition come about? "In ordinary circumstances," Wittgenstein observes, "these words and this picture have an application with which we are familiar. But if we suppose a case in which this application falls away we become as it were conscious for the first time of the nakedness of the words and the picture" (*PI*, §349). The same situation is apparent when Tolstoy becomes conscious for the first time of the meaninglessness of his life: "I could breathe, eat, drink, and sleep; indeed, I could not help but breathe, eat, drink, and sleep. But there was no life in me." Could it be, then, that Tolstoy lives a life that is separated from its form, a life that is stripped from its meaning, and left in its nakedness? Let me try to illustrate what I see as this nakedness of our words, and our lives, through another example. I am writing this paragraph while sitting in the New York Public Library. I am making a particular *use* of this place—I am writing here this paragraph. But this is also a favorite spot for tourists. They are taking pictures of the room, of me reading, or of themselves holding a book pretending to be reading. They are looking at the tables, the lamps, and the books with great marvel. Some are even taking the little pencils with which you write your book requests as souvenirs, while others are passing their inquisitive hands over the electricity sockets intended for personal computers. There are even some tourists at the entrance to the library who are acting according to a passage from Wittgenstein's notebook:

> People who are constantly asking 'why' are like tourists who stand in front of a building reading *Baedeker* [a popular German tourist guide], and are so busy reading the history of its construction, etc., that they are prevented from *seeing* the building. (*CV*, 40)

Now, I am not trying to suggest that Tolstoy is breezing through the question of the meaning of life as a tourist breezes through a handful of monuments in a single day. For Tolstoy, the meaning of life is not an object of curiosity but the most profound question there is. But I do want to claim that despite their sharp difference, the tourists Wittgenstein is talking about have an important affinity to Tolstoy when he writes: "Whenever my life came to a halt, the questions would arise: Why? And what next?" Notice *when* the question 'why' is aroused in him—*when his life comes to a halt*. In this condition, he can no longer *see* the meaning of his life. Then Tolstoy seems to ask, "What is life?" as Wittgenstein asks, "What is language?" without resolving this question "once and for all" and without discovering the "hidden essence." Because when you are separated from the ordinary life and the everyday language around you, you act like a tourist or like a philosopher. In Wittgenstein's *Investigations*, these two characters are closely related, "for philosophical problems arise when language *goes on holiday*" (*PI*, §38). A little later he explains this by saying that philosophical problems arise "when language is like an engine idling, not when it is doing work" (*PI*, §132). When you treat language as alienated from its possible use, when you are oblivious to what you can *do* with your words, then you lose your sense of direction. You act like those disoriented tourists in the middle of a foreign city: "A philosophical problem has the form: 'I don't know my way about'" (*PI*, §123). The same observation may help us to understand the way by which Tolstoy treats his life in the passage quoted above. When his life comes to a halt, it seems to be "on a holiday," "like an engine idling." He is unable to see how he is imbedded in the life around him. He does not know his way about. In this condition, the truth is, indeed, that life is meaningless.

3.3

Remember, however, that Wittgenstein testifies that he "cannot help respecting deeply" this hopeless search for the ultimate meaning of life, and he avows that he will not, for his life, "ridicule it" (*PO*, 44). It is not unlikely that he was thinking about Tolstoy when he made this comment. It is also important to mention that even though questions like, "What is the meaning of a word?" "What is language?" or "What is meaning?" seem to lead us to a mental cramp, Wittgenstein is neither ridiculing these questions nor is he asking us to abandon them. After all, these are the questions that remain at the center of his later philosophy. The answer to our questions concerning language and life would not be found in their disappearance. But we could still cope with these indispensable problems through a revision of the method by which we deal with them. This has to do with an insight Wittgenstein developed in his transitional period in the late 1920s: "The meaning of a question is the method of answering it . . . Tell me *how* you are searching, and I will tell you *what* you are searching for" (*PR*, 66–7). By reconsidering *how* you search for meaning in language and in life, you may also be able to reevaluate *what* it is exactly that you are trying to find.

In order to see how Wittgenstein altered his philosophical search, let me start in the beginning: "When they [my elders] named some object, and accordingly moved toward something, I saw this and I grasped that the thing was called by the sound they uttered when they meant to point it out" (*PI*, §1). In his first reaction to this passage from Augustine's *Confessions*, Wittgenstein transposes this idea to a situation in ordinary life:

> I send someone shopping. I give him a slip marked "five red apples." He takes the slip to the shopkeeper, who opens the drawer marked "apples;" then he looks up the word "red" in a table and finds the color sample opposite it; then he says the series of cardinal numbers— I assume that he knows them by heart—up to the words "five" and

for each number he takes an apple of the same color as the sample out of the drawer.—It is in this and similar ways that one operates with words.—"But how does he know where and how he is to look up the word 'red' and what he is to do with the word 'five'?"—Well, I assume that he *acts* as I have described. Explanations come to an end somewhere.—But what is the meaning of the word "five"?—No such thing was in question here, only how the word "five" is used. (*ibid.*)

In this spirit, I want to try and shift these considerations from Augustine's passage to Tolstoy's. Imagine that after Tolstoy finished writing about the meaninglessness of life, his wife Sofya entered the room and asked the great novelist to go to the market and buy five red apples. So he wrote on a slip of paper, "Five red apples," and put it in his pocket. What, then, is the relationship between the Tolstoy who wrote, "Life is meaningless," and the Tolstoy who wrote, "Five red apples"? Does the first Tolstoy somehow *correspond* to the second Tolstoy? Can the passage in which he maintains that life is meaningless *explain* the sense of the little note he wrote afterwards and his subsequent trip to the market? If one thinks that life is meaningless, does it necessarily entail that writing the note and getting the apples from the market are meaningless activities? But the note that says, "Five red apples" has a very simple use: Sofya wanted him to get some apples; Leo wrote the note so he would not forget, and he read it the next morning in the marketplace, where he purchased those five red apples, which his wife used later on in order to make the pie that the couple enjoyed after dinner. It is in this and similar ways that one lives his or her life. But why should one bother about dessert if life is meaningless? Well, I can assume that Tolstoy simply *acted* as Sofya asked him to act. In life, explanations come to an end somewhere, especially when your wife is involved. Imagine how Sofya would react if Leo refused to get the apples "because life is meaningless." Or imagine that Tolstoy returned from the market with five rotten apples. "I am really sorry," he told his wife, "I must have been contemplating the meaning of life while I picked them out." But if Tolstoy can still eat the apple pie (as he can still drink, breathe, and sleep), yet "there is no life" in him, is it to say that he is some kind of a lifeless eating machine? Does "life" or "the meaning of life" need to be understood as an "extra something" that we obtain on top of the mere fact of being alive? But again, what is the *meaning* of eating an apple pie? Well, such a thing was not in question here but only the place of this and other activities within the weave of a person's life.

3.4

A crucial aspect of Wittgenstein's philosophical method is "to teach you to pass from a piece of disguised nonsense to something that is patent nonsense" (*PI*, §464). In his writings from the last year and a half of his life, published under the title *On Certainty*, he employs this method in order to examine G. E. Moore's refutation of philosophical skepticism concerning the existence of an external world. Standing in a well-lit classroom, Moore raised his hand and said, "I know that this is a hand." According to him, this is a proof for the existence of at least one external object (his hand), and so it is a simple refutation of skepticism (Moore 1959). During his visit to New York, Wittgenstein had important discussions with Norman Malcolm about Moore's "proof." One of Wittgenstein's ideas that stayed in Malcolm's memory was that "an expression has meaning only in the stream of life" (Malcolm 1970: 93). You must see how a proposition like "I know that this is a hand" could be imbedded in your daily life. You need to ask when, in ordinary circumstances, are you actually inclined to say, "I know such and such," let alone, "I know that this is a hand?" Wittgenstein believes that such events are rare, if they exist at all (*OC*, §§11, 413). And even if you insist on imagining a strange situation in which a claim like "I know that this is a hand" is indeed "a move in one of our language-games," this proposition will then lose "everything that is philosophically astonishing" about it (*OC*, §622). At best, "I know that this is a hand" can only be a regular proposition in ordinary language. But it cannot function as a philosophical proof of something like the existence of the external world.

This approach may also help to reevaluate Tolstoy's claim that "the truth was that life is meaningless." Again, as a description of a stage in one's life, there is a great validity, even urgency, to his words. In this light, it is indeed a move in a language-game, and a pattern in the weave of Tolstoy's life. Many of us have moments of disorientation in life (some are more profound and some are momentary). When you feel that you do not know your way about in the stream of life, telling someone you trust that "life is meaningless" is somewhat similar to asking for directions in a foreign city. But seen from this perspective, Tolstoy's claim tends to lose "everything that is philosophically astonishing" about it. Similarly, Augustine's childhood memory about the way by which he learned to use language is not "philosophically astonishing" when you read it in the context of the *Confessions*, instead of as the opening scene of *Philosophical Investigations*. In fact, neither Augustine nor Tolstoy present these episodes from their own lives as particular pictures of the essence of human language or the essence of human life. It is the author of the *Investigations*, and the author of this book, who are responsible for this interpolation or "philosophication" of Augustine and Tolstoy's confessions.[23]

I need to note that Wittgenstein's aim in *On Certainty* is neither to dismiss the skepticism concerning the existence of the external world nor to affirm it. From the time of the *Tractatus*, Wittgenstein's position on this matter was very clear: "Skepticism is *not* irrefutable, but obviously nonsensical, when it tries to raise doubts where no questions can be asked" (*TLP*, §6.51). In *On Certainty*, you can see the other side of the same coin: the *refutation* of skepticism, exactly like skepticism itself, is obviously nonsensical, because it tries to assert certainty where no answer can be given. If the question disappears then the answer must vanish as well. Yet it took Wittgenstein three decades before he could explain his basic intuition by passing not only the assertion but also the refutation of skepticism from their position as disguised nonsense to a patent nonsense. In this spirit, I would like to stress that my aim here is neither to take lightly Tolstoy's skepticism concerning the existence of a meaningful life nor to make the opposite claim that the truth is that life is meaningful after all. We do not advance theses, or antitheses, in the philosophy of life. My only claim is that when you remove the question of meaning from the flux of life and place it in a kind of a "philosophical holiday," you may think that you make sense, but in fact you do not. To paraphrase Frege's dictum—"Never to ask for the meaning of a word in isolation, but only in the context of a proposition"—I could say the following: *Never look for meaning in isolation, but only in the context of a life* (Frege 1980: x).

Nonetheless, one can argue that there is something very rigid, almost intolerant, about Wittgenstein's position. It seems that a proposition like, "I know that this is a hand" makes perfect sense, since we can easily understand it, and Moore certainly knew what he meant when he uttered it. Moreover, this proposition appears to be "flamingly *obvious*," because it will be rather hopeless to try and doubt such a statement (Cavell 1979: 211). We are therefore tempted to believe that a proposition has two kinds of meanings: as if a sentence could still make sense and be true even though we are not sure about its application; as if a sentence has a "truth value" on the one hand, and then also a "use value" on top of it. Wittgenstein, however, shows us that the "meaning" of a proposition does not reside within the speaker, within the listener, within the proposition itself, or in some realm beyond the proposition. The meaning of the proposition emerges only from the context in which it is used. Outside its application in a language-game, separated from its place within a form of life, a proposition simply lacks sense. Full stop. As James Conant explains, the fact that a proposition *by itself* still *seems* to make sense is merely an appearance or a phantasm; it is simply this "old misunderstanding" about what it means to mean that Wittgenstein intends to cure us from (Conant 1998; *OC*, §393).

There is, however, another side to Wittgenstein's resolute view of meaning, which is even more counterintuitive than the first one. In the same way that we could be tempted to believe that something makes sense where in fact it is nonsensical, we are also very easily led to dismiss something as a piece of nonsense where in fact it is not. He illustrates this curious phenomenon with the following example:

> When I say that the orders "Bring me sugar" and "Bring me milk" make sense, but not the combination "Milk me sugar," that does not mean that the utterance of this combination of words has no effect. And if the effect is that the other person stares at me and gapes, I don't on that account call it the order to stare and gape, even if that was precisely the effect that I wanted to produce. (*PI*, §493)

There are a few things that you can milk, like cows, but sugar is definitely not one of them, while there are a few things that you can do with sugar, like pouring it, but you cannot milk it. Such a "combination of words," however, can still have a place in our language and an effect on our lives. Which is not to say that "Milk me sugar" is a sort of an "effective nonsense" in opposition to some kind of "ineffective nonsense." There are no different kinds of nonsense. If Wittgenstein achieves the effect that he wanted to produce by saying, "Milk me sugar," then it is simply no longer the nonsense that we took it to be. If by evoking a stanza from a poem I manage to produce a certain effect in my listener, then any attempt to claim for the nonsensicality of the poetic expression is in itself plain nonsense. It all depends on the context of our words, but not only within a proposition, as Frege claims. It depends on the context of the proposition itself within a situation, within a language-game, and within a form of life—where the words find their home. After all, if, in the course of a surgery, the doctor will say, "Bring me sugar," the nurse will probably stare at the surgeon and gape in the same manner that Wittgenstein's dinner companion stared at the philosopher and gaped when he told him, "Milk me sugar."

In these and similar cases, "when language-games change, then there is a change in concepts, and with the concepts the meaning of words change" (*OC*, §65). Such conceptual turns, however, are not restricted to the realm of language, since language is imbedded in our very lives: "What is called an alteration in concepts is of course not merely an alteration in what one says, but also in what one does" (*RPPI*, §910). Furthermore, we must also realize that even "what one does" never exists in isolation:

> How could human behavior be described? Surely only by sketching the actions of a variety of humans, as they are all mixed up together. What determines our judgment, our concepts and reactions, is not what *one* man is doing *now*, an individual action, but the whole hurly-burly of human actions, the background against which we see any action. (*Z*, §567)

We may therefore uncover the meaning of a particular aspect of our existence within the wide stream of life that it is a part of. We may also search for our place among the multiplicity of lives that surrounds us. We may also question or criticize certain elements as long as we pay close attention to their place within the hurly-burly of life. And we may even judge—simply by saying, "this is right" and "this is wrong"—as we come to acknowledge the form in which life is rooted. This will not reveal some sort of an essence still hidden from us. It will never lead to the answer that will be given once and for all. However, as Wittgenstein's approach enables him to present a new vision of language, it might also help us to begin to think anew about this life. For example, does it make sense to speak from the perspective of the *Investigations* about "*the* meaning of language" or only about "meaning *in* language"? Wittgenstein leads us to see the emptiness of the former and the labor required in order to reveal the latter. It is about time for people to recognize that although we are not going to find *the* meaning of life, we could certainly find meaning *in* life. Which is not to say that "the meaning of life" remains an ineffable mystery. "The absolute meaning of life" is not "something" of which we cannot speak. It is simply what we need to learn to pass from a piece of disguised nonsense to something that is patent nonsense.

3.5

"Our problems," Wittgenstein admits in the *Tractatus*, "are not abstract, but perhaps the most concrete that there are" (*TLP*, §5.5563). In the *Investigations*, he adds: "We are talking about the spatial and temporal phenomenon of language, not about some non-spatial, non-temporal phantasm" (*PI*, §108). We are dealing, if you like, with the actual uses, and occasional misuses, of our words. This method is not based on asking what the meaning of a word is but on our ability to see "how the words in question *are actually used in our language*" (*BB*, 56). "Have the use *TEACH* you the meaning," he demands (*RPPI*, §1013). In the *Investigations*, Wittgenstein goes as far as saying: "For a *large* class of cases—though not for all—in which we employ the word "meaning" it can be defined as this: the meaning of a word is its use in the language" (*PI*, §43). But we should not be tempted to reduce this idea into a theory or a thesis. We need to beware of "the dogmatism into which we fall so easily in doing philosophy" (*PI*, §131). Let me, then, try to explain how the dogma of "meaning as use" could be understood within the context of our considerations.

Use, *Gebrauch*, can also mean practice or exercise. To speak about the "use in the language" may therefore direct you back to the twenty-third remark in the *Investigations*: "The *speaking* of language is a part of an activity, or of a form of life." Language, *Sprache*, is a speaking, a *Sprechen*. What is at stake is always the use of language. This use, this speaking, is neither a state nor a possession but an *activity*.[24] If you think about language as a mirror of reality, now it becomes clear that our words cannot function as innocent bystanders that take a picture of the world. "Words," it is crucial to understand, "are also deeds" (*PI*, §546). If the whole world is a stage, then language is a player *on* this stage and not a mere spectator: "It is not a kind of *seeing* on our part; it is our *acting*, which lies at the bottom of the language-game" (*OC*, §204). The linguistic activity does not exist in a void but always within the space and time of our lives: "The *speaking* of language," let us remember once again, is not the whole activity, but only "a part of an activity," and this larger activity is exactly what Wittgenstein calls "form of life." Despite its centrality to the *Investigations*, language is far from being everything that is the case. In short, thinking about the idea that "the meaning of a word is its use in the language," without taking into consideration the way by which this use is weaved into our lives, misses an extremely important point. Wittgenstein was well aware of this possible misinterpretation, which he tackles in one of the first formulations of his later philosophy:

> Do I *understand* the word just by describing its application? Do I understand its point? Haven't I deluded myself about something important? At present, say, I know only how men use this word. But it might be a game, or a form of etiquette. I do not know why they behave in this way, how *language* meshes with their life. Is meaning then really only the use of a word? Isn't it the way this use meshes with our life? But isn't its use a part of our life? (*PG*, 65)

But if it is true that the use of language must be a part of our life, then the following question arises: What is this ephemeral entity that I call here, interchangeably, "life," "the mesh of life," "the stream of life," "the weave of life," and, ultimately, "the form of life"? One way of explaining what Wittgenstein means by all these expressions is to return to an early remark from a notebook he wrote during the First World War, in which he claims that one is "fulfilling the purpose of existence" when one "no longer needs to have any purpose except to live" (*NB*, 73). Notice how this early attitude toward life goes along the lines of his later attitude toward language. Life, like language, is not an abstract or theoretical phenomenon, but the most concrete thing there is. We are talking about the spatial and temporal phenomenon of life and not about some non-spatial, non-temporal phantasm. A form of life is neither a possession nor a state but, indeed, an *activity*—a *vita activa*. *Living*, which the young Wittgenstein takes to be the only fulfillment of the purpose of existence, seems to have a secret affinity with what he will later call *speaking*: the *speaking* of language ("*Das* Sprechen *der Sprache*"), the *living* of life. After all, it is our *acting* that lies at the bottom of a form of life. A form of life is what we participate in and not what we correspond to. We can therefore see now how our understanding of a *form of life* is incomplete before we also consider what I would like to call the *life of form*. If a life has a form, then this form must have a life. A form of life is neither static nor eternal; a form of life is a stream of life. What gives a form its life is the way by which we use its powers and exercise its possibilities. If forms are not *lived*, they can simply become obsolete and get forgotten, like language-games; they become meaningless or dead.

"We don't want to say that meaning is a special experience, but that it isn't anything which happens, or happens to us, but something that we do, otherwise it would be just dead" (*PG*, 156). So maybe, one will suggest, Tolstoy thought that life is meaningless because he expected to find a special experience of meaning. But meaning, Wittgenstein explains, is not something that happens to us but simply what we do: writing that life is meaningless, going to the market to buy some apples, baking a pie and eating it, talking about your day, praying, hoping, loving—all these form patterns in the weave of a life. The meaning of any of these patterns, like the meaning of any word that we use in our language, is not something extraordinary, something extra on top of ordinary life or everyday language. It is simply what we do—we speak, we live. How we speak and live is the meaning of language and life.

Wittgenstein helps you to see that there is nothing sacred, sublime, mysterious, or occult about the meaning of words: "When I think in language, there aren't 'meanings' going through my mind in addition to the verbal expressions: the language is itself the vehicle of thought" (*PI*, §329). When the linguistic engine is idling, words are a vehicle of nonsense, of idle talk; but the very same engine could also become the vehicle of meaningful thought. "Meaning," however, is neither the fuel of the engine nor the destination of the vehicle, but it is the very movement, work, or activity, while the engine is in gear. In this way, meaning is taken by Wittgenstein to be inseparable from the use of language:

> You say: the point isn't the word, but its meaning, and you think of the meaning as a thing of the same kind as the word, though also different from the word. Here the word, there the meaning. The money, and the cow that you can buy with it. (But contrast: money, and its use.) (*PI*, §120)

Notice that Wittgenstein is not disagreeing with his imaginary interlocutor: indeed, what is important is not the word but its meaning. What he contests is the idea that meaning could be seen as separate from the word itself: "Here the word, there the meaning." To ask for the meaning of a word is like asking for the value of a 100 dollar bill. Yes, I might use this money in order to buy a cow, but this is not to say that the cow corresponds to my money. It is very interesting to find in an earlier version of this remark the following list of a few of the things that you can use your money for: "Sometimes a material object, sometimes the right to a seat in the theatre, or a title, or fast travel, or life, etc." (*PG*, 63).[25] In the same manner, you no longer need to think that "meaning" is something that correlates to a word: the concept "cow" and the physical cow that you denote with the word. In the same way that there is a multiplicity of things that I can use my money for, there are always different things that I can do with a single word: sometimes I call "cow" while pointing to it in order to teach my child the meaning of this word; sometimes I shout "cow" when driving with my wife in a car and suddenly I see a cow in the middle of the road; sometimes I say "cow" when the counterperson at the deli asks me whether I would like to buy cheese made from goat's milk or cow's milk; sometimes I whisper "cow" to a friend in a party while we glance at a person who is devouring all the *hors d'oeuvre*, and so on. Even though these examples seem to be so insignificant and mundane, or even profane, the meaning of the word "cow" cannot be separated from this multiplicity of possible uses.[26]

One may take Tolstoy to say the following: the point isn't life, but its meaning. And this is true. But can this meaning exist apart from living itself? Here a life, there a meaning? Wittgenstein shows you an alternative way of looking at this issue. When you live your life, there are no 'meanings' that accompany your activities, like halos or shadows. The meaning of life is not going through your mind in addition to living itself. Living is itself the vehicle of the thought of life. Although "philosophers very often talk about investigating, analyzing, the meaning of words," Wittgenstein tries to make sure that you will "not forget that a word hasn't got a meaning given to it, as it were, by a power independent of us" (*BB*, 27–8). It is us, those who speak, who give our language its meaning. And it is us, those who live, who make this life into a meaningful experience. Meaning dwells in the midst of our life.

3.6

In the *Tractatus*, Wittgenstein asserts that a picture "is laid against reality like a scale [*maβstab*]" (*TLP*, §2.1512). In the *Investigations*, he realizes that this simile does not explain anything but is in itself in need of explanation:

> "Put a ruler [*maβstab*] against this body; it does not say that the body is of such-and-such a length. Rather is it in itself—I should like to say—dead, and achieves nothing of what thought achieves."— It is as if we had imagined that the essential thing about a living man was the outward form. Then we made a lump of wood in that form, and were abashed to see the stupid block, which hadn't even any similarity to a living being. (*PI*, §430)

There is definitely something missing from the relationship between language and reality. That a proposition and a fact share a logical form cannot be the end of the story. One could say that the form of language is like an effigy that has the outward form of a man, but it still lacks the spark of life. As a result, the logical form achieves nothing but a *dead correspondence*, so to speak. This should not lead us, however, to the nihilistic claim that language is separated from reality, that we cannot mean things in the world with our words. This is not what Wittgenstein says. But he still insists that we must reconsider what it means to mean: "When we mean something, it's like going up to someone, it's not having a dead picture (of any kind). We go up to the thing we mean" (*PI*, §455). To mean something, to reach out to it, is like, I want to say, *touching* it. But touching is something that only a living being can do. A living being can touch another living being or even something that is not alive, like a stone, but even if a stone is placed on top of another stone, it is not, properly speaking, "touching" it.[27] Hence, in order for our words to be like a "picture that touches reality," language must be, in some sense, *alive* (*TLP*, §2.1515). If a sign is not alive, it cannot *signify*. This "aliveness" is a key that can help us to unlock Wittgenstein's understanding of meaning.

"Every sign *by itself* seems dead. *What* gives it life?—In use it is *alive*. Is life breathed into it there?—Or is the *use* its life?" (*PI*, §432). This remark, by itself, seems rather peculiar. But when you compare it with its numerous variations in the preliminary manuscripts that led to the composition of the *Investigations*, it becomes alive and meaningful. In an early draft, we find Wittgenstein contemplating Frege's idea that a sentence is the expression of a thought. "In every case," he remarks, "what is meant by 'thought' is the *living* element in the sentence, without which it is dead, a mere succession of sounds or series of written shapes" (*PG*, 107). In a second text, he explains the nature of this living element: "But if we had to name anything which is the life of the sign, we should have to say that it was its *use*" (*BB*, 4). These considerations lead to the claim that our signs are, in a sense, arbitrary: "The words used don't matter, of course; they could be 'X' and 'Z'. But what must we do with the words to give them some sort of life? We must explain them, *use* them" (*PO*, 362–3). This use, Wittgenstein further clarifies, cannot take place in a void but always within a context: "We thus would have invented a surrounding for the word, a game in which its use is a move. It does not matter whether in practice the word has a place in a game, but what matters is that we have a game, that a life is given to it" (*WLC*, 124). "Only in the system," he can therefore conclude, "has the sign any life" (*Z*, §146). A close examination of these remarks in conjunction with the idea that "the meaning of a word is its use in the language" reveals a curious fact. *For Wittgenstein, to say that a sign is alive and to say that it is meaningful amounts to the same thing. The meaning of a sign is its life, and the life of a sign is its meaning. The words 'life' and 'meaning', 'alive' and 'meaningful', are used interchangeably.*

But if life and meaning are one, then "the meaning of life" could be reduced to the seemingly redundant expression, "the life of life." Not incidentally, one can actually find Augustine searching in his *Confessions* for exactly this "life of life" or *vitae vita*.[28] In this expression, however, the first life and the second life are not the same. The second life, *vita*, signifies for Augustine something like the mere fact of being alive, which animals and humans share with one another. On the other hand, the first life, *vitae*, is something completely different. This is the true, eternal, and happy life. It is this second use of the word "life" that stands at the center of Augustine's quest in his *Confessions*. Even though he knows that he is factually alive, this life is still a certain kind of a "living death" for him. It is not in mere life, but in the life of life, that he finds redemption.[29]

In a very similar manner, Tolstoy cannot help but breathe, eat, drink, and sleep, but there is still no *life* in him. Such a lifeless or meaningless life, I would like to suggest, is not unlike a nonsensical proposition. In the same way that Augustine and Tolstoy show us the threat of a life that seems to be alive though in fact it is dead or meaningless, Wittgenstein never tires of showing us how a sign, which appears to have a life, can also be rather dead and how a proposition that seems to have sense might be nothing but nonsense in disguise. But this, as we have seen, is only one side of the story. In the course of their confessions, both Augustine and Tolstoy manage to permeate their empty existence with meaning, to saturate it with life. Similarly, Wittgenstein also shows us how a proposition that at first glance may appear to be nonsensical can still have a use and therefore a sense, and how we could easily bring to life a concept that looks rather dead. There is no way, however, to predetermine the life of signs or the signs of life.

What, then, gives life to our language? And what gives meaning to our life? Could it be a gift bestowed from above? Is there a divine entity that "breathed life" into our signs and our bodies? Wittgenstein, a dedicated reader of Augustine and Tolstoy, and a deeply religious person who once wrote that "the meaning of life, i.e. the meaning of the world, we can call God," could easily leave it at that (*NB*, 73). Instead, his philosophy offers a new way of thinking about this old problem. If a sign is not isolated, but used within a context, then it can be alive. And if it is alive, then it is meaningful. In a similar way, we can now see that when the *living* of life is a part of an activity, or of a form of life, then the *meaning* of this life is at hand.

But I also want to say that Wittgenstein is not simply rejecting in his later philosophy Augustine and Tolstoy's link between God, meaning, and life, on the condition that you recognize that for these three thinkers "God" is not an entity that lies *beyond* life bestowing on it absolute sense or invariant moral norms from above. As Wittgenstein shows in his "Lecture on Ethics," such a metaphysical God, in its "absolute sense," is nonsensical (*PO*, 42–3). But "God" may also be a sign that is used in a completely different way, this is to say, as a sign for the very life of life. In Tolstoy, this radical approach to the notion of God is the most apparent, since his eventual discovery of meaning arises from his appreciation of the ordinary life in his village, of the everyday activity of the peasants around him. At the end of his confession, Tolstoy meshes with this simple form of life and not with some sort of a mystical divinity. He could therefore claim that his faith in God has nothing to do with the acceptance of a dogma, because "faith" is for him simply "the knowledge of the meaning of human life" (Tolstoy 1983: 61). In a way, he brings God back from its metaphysical position to its home in the everyday. He can therefore crystallize this crucial idea in a definitive formulation: "To know God and to live come to one and the same thing. God is life" (*ibid.*: 74). Or, if you wish, *Deus sive Vita*. But this, again, is not a metaphysical claim. It is, like Spinoza's "*Deus sive Natura*" and Wittgenstein's "The world and life are one," the threshold to a new ethics.

Chapter 4

Philosophy

4.1

At the end of the *Tractatus Logico-Philosophicus*, Wittgenstein states that anyone who understands him eventually recognizes that the propositions of his book are nonsensical. If you understand *him*, rather than try to understand such nonsensical propositions, then you can use these propositions "as steps—to climb up beyond them" (*TLP*, §6.54). You must therefore "throw away the ladder" after you have climbed up on it, and then, by "transcending these propositions," he promises that you "will see the world aright" (*ibid.*). But in a notebook entry from 1930, a decade after the publication of the *Tractatus*, Wittgenstein revisits the metaphor of the ladder and arrives at what seems to be a radically different conclusion:

> I might say: if the place I want to get to could only be reached by way of a ladder, I would give up trying to get there. For the place I really have to get to is a place I must already be at now. Anything that I might reach by climbing a ladder does not interest me. (*CV*, 7)

You might assume that by reading the *Tractatus* you are really climbing a ladder that takes you to a higher vantage point, a place from which you could see the world rightly. I believe, however, that when Wittgenstein writes, a decade later, that he is not interested in any place that can be reached by climbing a ladder, he does not go *against* his early thought but *elucidates* it for us and maybe even for himself. The *Tractatus*, he seems to say, is by no means a ladder. What the book is intended to do, in fact, is to help you lose this false pretence that it is possible to stand above the world by means of such a ladder. If you think that the book is a ladder, then you need *to throw this ladder away*. You could see the world aright—*not* because you ascend on a ladder, but exactly because you realize that ladder climbing is not what you need to be doing. If the propositions of the book are indeed nonsensical, then you are climbing a ladder of nonsense. You cannot get any higher by climbing this ladder made of thin air. Yet you can better realize, after reading the book with understanding, the place in which you are already standing.[30]

These considerations will help me to come to terms with the consequences of Cora Diamond and James Conant's "resolute" reading of the *Tractatus*. One of the main features of this interpretation is the insistence that when Wittgenstein writes, at the end of his book, that "what we cannot speak about we must pass over in silence," he is not trying to claim that there is *something* about which we cannot speak (*TLP*, §7). It is misleading to read the *Tractatus*, the two scholars suggest, as if there are certain things that we can speak about in language, while there are other things that we know exist, but alas, we are incapable of speaking about them. "Propositions," Wittgenstein insists, "can express nothing that is higher" (*TLP*, §6.42). The *Tractatus*, therefore, is not offering us a metaphysical image of an inside and an outside; of a world and that which lies beyond. The point of the book is not really to say that "the world has this in it, and this, but not that" (*TLP*, §5.61). "For the point of the book," Wittgenstein explains in the letter to von Ficker, "is ethical" (*WSP*, 94). In short, you are not asked to *believe* in something but to *do* something—to be silent when this silence is needed. What you cannot speak about, what you must pass over in silence, is not a thing but a temptation. Although "many others today are just gassing [*schwefeln*]," Wittgenstein takes his achievement to lie in his ability "to put everything firmly into place by being silent about it" (*ibid.*).

The problem, however, is that we constantly speak about what we cannot speak about. We *can* participate in this idle talk if we want to. But we can also do something else: we can say, like Bartleby the Scrivener, "I would prefer not to" (Melville 2004: 47). Wittgenstein prefers not to speak—*not* because he knows that there is a realm of things that exists somewhere yet he is incapable of speaking about it, but simply because he comes to see the nonsensicality of many of the things that a lot of people say. After all, being silent is not the same as being mute. A person who is mute does not speak *because* of the fact that he *cannot* speak; a person who remains silent does not speak *despite* the fact that he *can* speak. Being silent, like speaking, should be understood as a mark of power, of potentiality, rather than as a mark of impotence or powerlessness. Only those who possess the power of speech can also possess the power of silence. If Aristotle sees humans as the living beings that have the ability to use language, then Wittgenstein reminds us that these living beings also have the ability *not* to use language. Without this second ability neither our language nor our life would be of any value.[31]

By following this line of investigation, we can now establish a link between Wittgenstein's resolute view of language and what I would like to call "the resolute view of life." This is an attempt to imagine a form of life in which "you don't stand on stilts or on a ladder but on your bare feet" (*CV*, 33). It is a life that is no longer tempted by the fantasy of ascent, by what you can reach by climbing a ladder. It is a life that knows that what is at stake is always living itself, rather than a life hereafter. What is higher is of no interest to the resolute view of life. Again, this is not to say that there is an ineffable realm outside the reach of the language that we speak and the life that we live. The question, remember, is not what we believe but what we do and what we do not do—how we live our life. The question is an ethical one. Even though you *can* stand on stilts, and even though you *can* look for what is higher, as many others still do, you come to recognize the vacuity of this endeavor, and you simply prefer not to partake in it. By throwing away the stilts or the ladder, you see the emptiness of that which "lies beyond this life." By standing on your own bare feet, you face the fullness of an immanent life.[32]

A standard reading of the *Tractatus* offers a metaphysical picture of a closed realm, its definitive limits, and its unreachable and ineffable beyond. We are therefore led to assume that what lies outside some-how *constitutes the meaning of the inside*. This attitude can be perfectly applied to what we understand as "life" as well as "the world." Here is how Wittgenstein phrases this metaphysical tendency in his *Tractatus*: "The sense of the world must lie outside the world;" "The solution to the riddle of life in space and time lies *outside* space and time"

(*TLP*, §§6.41, 6.4312). These claims lead us to think that *in* the world, as *within* life, "everything is as it is, and everything happens as it does happen: *in* it no value exists—and if it did exist, it would have no value" (*TLP*, §6.41). The thought of the outside, which seems to retain a mystical and redemptive notoriety, is precisely the illusion that a resolute view of language and life tries to reveal as such.

One of the best manifestations for this resolute attitude is to be found again toward the end of the *Tractatus*:

> The solution to the problem of life is seen in the vanishing of the problem. (Is not this the reason why those who have found after a long period of doubt that the sense of life became clear to them have then been unable to say what constituted that sense?) (*TLP*, §6.521)

"The sense of life," so it seems, requires no explanations and no definitions. It takes care of itself. You might assume then that by reading the *Tractatus* with understanding you could solve the problem of life and make it vanish once and for all; that you could finally find the sense of life, even though you will not be able to talk about your discovery with other people. Nevertheless, in another crucial remark from Wittgenstein's notebook from 1930, after he returned to do philosophy, one finds what appears to be a straightforward criticism of the conclusion of his early work:

> If anyone should think he has solved the problem of life and feel like telling himself that everything is quite easy now, he can see that he is wrong just by recalling that there was a time when this "solution" had not been discovered; but it must have been possible to live *then* too. (*CV*, 4)

Once again, I would like to suggest that Wittgenstein is actually trying here to clarify his earlier formulation rather than to negate it. From the perspective of a resolute view of life, if the sense of life becomes clear to me, then I do not possess *something* that the one who still lives in doubt lacks. The difference is merely that I acknowledge that the attempt to find a "solution" to the problem of life, to discover the definitive sense of life, or the ultimate meaning of life, is nonsensical. It is not that I have the answer, but I cannot tell you what it is.

My only secret is that I have no secret. Within the framework of the *Tractatus*, you can speak about facts in the world by means of propositions of natural science. But as you may recall, "we feel that even if *all possible* scientific questions be answered, the problems of life have still not been touched at all" (*TLP*, §6.52). Although the *Tractatus* shows you a way by which your words could reach out and touch reality, it does not have even the pretence that it is within its power to touch the "problem of life." The moment Wittgenstein touches this "problem" in his book, it immediately melts into air *together with the book itself.*

Let me draw your attention once again to the remark quoted above about the time before the "solution" to the problem of life had been discovered. Here is how it continues:

> And it is the same in the study of logic. If there were a "solution" to the problems of logic (philosophy) we should only need to caution ourselves that there was a time when they had not been solved (and even at that time people must have known how to live and think.) (*CV*, 4)

We can therefore discern a direct link between the resolute view of language and the resolute view of life. Wittgenstein wonders how one could live and think before the solution to logical (or, I could add, ethical) problems was found. Needless to say, it is impossible to represent such a turn with "before" and "after" pictures, like an advertisement for magical diet pills. The *Tractatus* is not trying to show you the solution to your problems in seven easy steps by teaching you how to live and how to think. The resolute view of language and of life is not trying to reach a moment in which one "will feel like telling himself that everything is quite easy now." If anything, it is trying to show you "how little is achieved" when you find the final solution to philosophical problems (*TLP*, Preface). From this perspective, silence is not meant to make you aware of that which remains unsaid but to make you attend to the little that *is* said.[33]

4.2

In *Philosophical Investigations*, Wittgenstein indicates toward the need to "profanate" our words: "If the words 'language,' 'experience,' 'world,' have a use, it must be as humble a one as that of the words 'table,' 'lamp,' 'door'" (*PI*, §97). When our concepts are detached from their simple use, they transform into a kind of sacred or metaphysical entities. To "profanate" our language is simply to insist on asking: "Is the word ever actually used in this way in the language-game which is its original home?" (*PI*, §116). Let me clarify what I mean when I speak about "sacred" words and the "profanation" of language. For Roman jurists, a thing was considered to be profane if humans could freely touch it, use it, and exchange it. A sacred object was banned from this free use of man and so it was reserved for the Gods. Accordingly, "profanation" was a process through which things were brought back from their sacred and unusable position to their free employment by humanity (Agamben 2007: 73). In a revealing moment where Wittgenstein elucidates his philosophical project you can see exactly this act of linguistic profanation: "What *we* do is to bring words back from their metaphysical to their everyday use" (*PI*, §116). There are no metaphysical concepts but only concepts used in a metaphysical way. The sacred is sacred only because we make it so. In this vein, I could say that what *we* try to do here is to achieve a similar profanation of our approach to life. We want to bring life back from its sacred or metaphysical position to its home in the everyday. Once again, this link between language and life is not coincidental. As Stanley Cavell (via Heidegger) explains, you cannot "bring words back" without "*leading* them back, shepherding them," because "the behavior of words is not something separated from our lives, those of us who are native to them, in mastery of them. The lives themselves have to return" (Cavell 1989: 35).

"Philosophy," Wittgenstein writes, "simply puts everything before us, and neither explains nor deduces anything.—Since everything lies open to view there is nothing to explain. For what is hidden, for example, is of no interest to us" (*PI*, §126). The duty of philosophy is therefore not "to dig down to the ground" but "to recognize the ground that lies before us as the ground" (*RFM*, 333). From this perspective, we could see that it is not only the ladder, but also the shovel, that Wittgenstein's philosophy enables us to throw behind. But what, exactly, is this ground that lies before us? What do we see when we look at what lies open to view? If we should have no interest in what is hidden, how do we come to see what is *not* hidden? It still seems that "the aspects of things that are most important for us are hidden because of their simplicity and familiarity" (*PI*, §129). We have eyes, but we cannot see; we have ears, but we cannot hear. Yet what is it that needs to be seen and to be heard? In order to answer this question, "let us imagine a theater:"

> The curtain goes up and we see a man alone in a room, walking up and down, lightening a cigarette, sitting down, etc. so that suddenly we are observing a human being from outside in a way that ordinarily we can never observe ourselves; it would be like watching a chapter of biography with our own eyes—surely this would be uncanny and wonderful at the same time. We should be observing something more wonderful than anything a playwright could arrange to be acted or spoken on the stage: *life itself*.—But then we do see this every day without its making the slightest impression on us! (*CV*, 4, emphasis added)

Wittgenstein's theater tries to illuminate something that is devoid of any metaphysical pretensions, something utterly profane and ordinary. After all, "does what is ordinary always make the *impression* of ordinariness?" (*PI*, §600). Our everyday life, the life that always lies before us, which remains hidden exactly because of its simplicity and familiarity, is presented in Wittgenstein's theater as a world saturated with meaning and importance. In a related remark he explains that the viewers in this theater, ourselves, can therefore be "awaken to wonder" by realizing how "things are placed right in front of our eyes, not covered by any veil" (*CV*, 5–6). This experience of wonder may evoke a sort of a profane illumination of living itself, because it is not some sort of a strange or unfamiliar form of life that we see on the stage of Wittgenstein's theater. We are not supposed to "learn anything *new*" from this performance, but simply "to *understand* something that is already in plain view. For *this* is what we seem in some sense not to understand" (*PI*, §89). It is the strangeness, the uncanniness, of our ordinary lives that we must confront now.

"If you want to go down deep," Wittgenstein therefore advises, "you do not need to travel far; indeed, you don't have to leave your most immediate and familiar surroundings" (*CV*, 50). If you assume that it is a simple task to see what is right in front of your eyes, in your most familiar surroundings, Wittgenstein replies: "How small a thought it takes to fill a whole life!" (*ibid.*). How easy it is to lose your attention to this "small thought" of life—to all those words, deeds, feelings, people, situations, places, occasions, questions, problems, facts, tasks and so on and so forth that saturate your daily existence. This attention to life is, of course, not something that you can see in a flash, not something that is given once and for all. It is, rather, a continuous labor. "But then," we hear Wittgenstein's voice of temptation, "we will never get to the end of our job!" which brings Wittgenstein's voice of correction to reply: "Of course not, because it has no end" (Monk 1990: 325). And so, as the Greeks used to say, we spend our whole life learning how to live.

4.3

"The work of the philosopher consists in assembling reminders for a particular purpose" (*PI*, §127). You constantly need to remind yourself of how you actually live and speak. Echoing Plato's conception of learning as remembering, Wittgenstein admits that "learning philosophy is *really* recollecting," yet he explains that it is so not because we need to remind ourselves of some eternal forms that exist deep down or up high, but simply because we need to "remember that we really used words in this way" (*PO*, 179). It is not the recollection of some ideal language or life, but the recollection of the way you speak and the way you live in this world, here and now, which is the essence of the philosophical practice. Like Augustine's famous observation concerning time, you can now see that language and life are good examples for the kind of things that we certainly "know when no one asks us, but no longer know when we are supposed to give an account of"—which is precisely the reason why these are the things "that we need to *remind* ourselves of" (*PI*, §89).

A concrete example will help me to show this method of recollection at work. If you forget for a second the way language is actually used, you might be convinced that "sense" is a kind of "an atmosphere accompanying the word, which it carried with it into every kind of

application" (*PI*, §117). In order to avoid this metaphysical temptation, Wittgenstein reminds you:

> If, for example, someone says that the sentence "This is here"
> (saying which he points to an object in front of him) makes sense
> to him, then he should ask himself in what special circumstances
> this sentence is actually used. There it does make sense. (*ibid.*)

The curious phenomenon that Wittgenstein points at came to
be known among some linguists as "indexicals" and by others as
"shifters"—words that change their reference according to the event
in which they are uttered. *This* and *here* in Wittgenstein's example are
such shifters. Think also about the words *I* and *now*, which make sense
only because, for instance, it is *I* who is speaking right *now*. In one of
his lectures Wittgenstein explained this problem in the following
terms: "Take the expression 'I', 'here', 'now.' What is 'now'? A moment
in time. But which moment of time is it?—So also: What is 'here'?
Which place is it? Who is 'I'? A person. But which person is it?" (*PO*,
319). And compare with this other witty remark: "If from one day to
the next you promise: 'Tomorrow I will come and see you' —are you
saying the same thing every day, or every day something different?"
(*PI*, §226).

There is something quite disturbing about the idea of words that
do not have a specific and fixed reference, because their meaning
is, so to speak, shifting according to the context in which they are
being used. But even if these ephemeral shifters seem disquieting,
you may still believe that they are only the exception to the rule; that
in ordinary cases, most words, like "hand" or "tree," do have a specific
meaning that is somewhat static and definite and is independent
of their specific employment in actual language. But if you follow
Wittgenstein in this crucial issue, you see that his philosophy suggests
an even more radical idea: *The whole of language is, essentially, a language of shifters.* "Meaning" is not something that exists outside the
event in which we use our words. The flux of life, the constant change
of contexts, and our infinitely various linguistic tools always shift the
meaning of our words hither and thither. Of course, when you use

language in everyday life your words *do* have concrete meaning, and you do not feel that it is shifting. If, in the course of a conversation, I look at the sculpture in front of me and say, "This is here," then this sentence could have a very clear meaning, even though it may shift if I will point to something else or stand in a different place. What matters is what I point to right now, right here.

I therefore want to say that the speaking of language is not something that can be understood from the viewpoint of eternity, since words do not have a fixed meaning forever. But I also do not see language from the perspective of time, since the meaning of my words at the moment of speaking them does not need to account for the way I used them yesterday or will use them tomorrow. For Wittgenstein, the question is what do I *do* with my words, not what I *did* or *will do* with them. As a result, his vision of language, in both the "early" and the "later" philosophy, has a certain air of timelessness. Reading his remarks, you rarely get the sense that language declines, or progresses, changes, or remains the same, since all these valuations have to do with the idea of a linear passage of time. There is very little attention to the "history" of language or to its "future."[34] But this is not to say that Wittgenstein was oblivious to the question of temporality. His view of the matter is stated already in the *Tractatus*: "If we take eternity to mean not infinite temporal duration but timelessness, then eternal life belongs to those who live in the present" (*TLP*, §6.4311). Accordingly, one may say that, for Wittgenstein, language belongs to those who speak in the present. "Only a man who lives not in time but in the present is happy," as only a man who speaks not in time but in the present situation can make sense of his words (*NB*, 74). Language and life have no specific direction or purpose that unravels over time, as they have no particular essence or definition that remains constant as time passes. The time of our language and our life is always the time of now. And this is why Wittgenstein's philosophy is not a remembrance of things past but a remembrance of things present. Which is not to say that time for him is empty, homogenous, or insignificant. On the contrary, every moment in which you speak and live is like a small door through which language and life enter into this world.[35]

4.4

Wittgenstein's distinctive comportment toward time may become clearer if we compare it with his matching perception of space. We have seen how a resolute reading of the *Tractatus* helps us to put aside the traditional picture of an inside, an outside, and the limits that separate between the two, and instead enables us to imagine what I call here the immanence of language and life. Nevertheless, there are still two important propositions from the book that one must come to terms with. The first is the statement that "the aim of the book is to draw a limit to thought, or rather—not to thought, but to the expression of thought" (*TLP*, Preface). The second is the assertion that "*the limits of my language* mean the limits of my world" (*TLP*, §5.6). If there is no division into an inside and an outside, how then are we to understand the place of the limit, boundary, or threshold (*Grenze*) in Wittgenstein's philosophy? Why should one draw a limit if there is nothing that lies in the beyond? What is the sense of a world that is not simply a whole, but a "limited whole" (*TLP*, §6.45)?

I think that a possible lead may be found in another remark that appears toward the end of the *Tractatus*, where the idea of the limit is contrasted with the idea of limitlessness: "Our life has no end [*endlos*] in just the same way in which our visual field has no limits [*grenzen-los*]" (*TLP*, §6.4311). Once again, this hermetic statement cannot solve the puzzle before it undergoes some serious clarifications. Therefore, I should actually begin by asking the following question: in what way is our visual field limitless? Let me rephrase: How far can the human eye see? The answer is that this is a tricky question. There is no specific limit beyond which you cannot see. The only question is whether the light from a distant star can manage to reach your eye or not, which has nothing to do with physiology but with simple physics. In a sense, the only thing that the human eye can see is something that is in zero distance from it. Our brain interprets the visual sensation as objects that are near or far away, even though it does not know that the light from certain objects traveled a few light-years and others traveled just a few feet. So if this is the way by which the visual field has no limits, then you could see that life is endless not because you can travel far but because you don't have to leave your most immediate and familiar surroundings in order to see what anyhow lies open to view.

Again, there is a statement from Wittgenstein's "threshold period," after he returned to do work in philosophy in the late 1920s, that will help us to see the cryptic remark concerning the endlessness of our lives in a better light. Here we find a short discussion of a drawing from Ernst Mach's *Analysis of Sensations*, where the physicist depicts his visual field in such a way that "the so-called blurredness of the figures near the edge of the visual field was reproduced by a blurredness (in a quite different sense) in the drawing" (*PR*, 267). In Mach's drawing, you see a room with a bookcase to the left and a window in the front. There is a man sitting on an armchair at the center of the room with his legs stretched out. You can detect his right hand, holding the pencil with which this very drawing is purportedly made. You may also notice half of a Prussian moustache, complete with the left half of a snubbed-nose. Then, in the periphery, you can even trace the fuzzy socket of the eye that its visual field this drawing is supposed to reproduce (Mach 1996: 19). Wittgenstein, however, fiercely objects to this rendering: "No, you can't make a visual picture of our visual image," because "without this 'blurredness' the limitlessness of visual space isn't conceivable" (*PR*, 268). For the form of the visual field is surely not as Mach takes it to be. In other words, our visual field seems to be limitless because we cannot *see* the limits, let alone *represent* them. Our visual field has no limits since "it is less clear at the edges than toward the middle" (*PR*, 267). In another remark, Wittgenstein explains why we are, so to speak, blind to our own blindness:

> We do not notice that we see space perspectively or that our visual field is in some sense blurred towards the edges. It doesn't strike us and never can strike us because it is *the* way we perceive. We never give it a thought and it's impossible we should, since there is nothing that contrasts with the form of our world. (*PR*, 80)

Yet this "form of our world," Wittgenstein further explains, is the form of *our* world—it is something that we consider as "the given," what we "never long to escape from," and what "we take as a matter of course"—in short, it precisely what Wittgenstein calls, here and elsewhere, "*life*" (*ibid.*). The form of our world is the form of our life.

Reading the above remarks on the background of the *Tractatus* enables me to draw the following conclusions: It seems that however I may conceive of the limits of my world, which Wittgenstein connects to the limits of my language as well as the limits of thought, these limits are indistinguishable from the limits of my life. The claim that "our life has no end in just the same way in which our visual field has no limits" seems to suggest that our life has no end just because we cannot *see* its end and because we are incapable of *representing* it. Only in this way can one fully understand why "death is not an event in life" and why "we do not live to experience death" (*TLP*, §6.4311). In the same way that we cannot represent the blurred limits of our visual field, we cannot explain the threshold of our lives in a clear and distinct way. As Edgar Allen Poe knew very well, "The boundaries which divide Life from Death are at best shadowy and vague" (Poe 1984: 261). The idea that life has no end has therefore nothing to do with living forever, without death, in just the same way that the claim that our visual field has no limits does not mean that I can see every star from any distant galaxy or that I can see what happens behind my back. This is also not to deny that we do set numerous boundaries to the conduct of our lives. It is not hard to understand why "a living thing can be healthy, strong and fruitful only when bounded by a horizon" (Nietzsche 1997: 63). Nevertheless, we are prevented from making a clear distinction between what is within and what is beyond this horizon, because the experience of the limit is an experience of disorientation, of a limbo; it is a zone of indetermination. And so, even though the *Tractatus* suggests a very sharp distinction between what can be said and what cannot be said, a threshold, for Wittgenstein, is not something that you can actually account for by making clear-cut separations. Even though philosophy is here to transform thoughts that are "cloudy and indistinct" into clear thoughts with "sharp boundaries," there is no indication that one can *say* what are the boundaries of our thoughts (*TLP*, §4.112). In conclusion, the pretence that we can actually see, draw, or speak about such limits is one of those futile tasks that we need to throw away behind us after we read the *Tractatus* with understanding.[36]

And this is exactly what Wittgenstein did in his later philosophy, where he breaks with Frege's attempt to compare a concept to an area and to claim "that an area with vague boundaries cannot be called an area at all:"

> This presumably means that we cannot do anything with it.—But is it senseless to say: "Stand roughly there"? Suppose that I were standing with someone in a city square and said that. As I say it I do not draw any kind of boundary, but perhaps point with my hand— as if I were indicating a particular spot. (*PI*, §71)

No, the ability to draw sharp boundaries to the concept of language is not the condition for the possibility to speak meaningfully, as the inability to have clear and distinct limits to our conception of life does not deter us from living a meaningful life. When it comes to concepts like language or life, we do not necessarily *want* to draw sharp boundaries. Recall that Wittgenstein maintains that "the concept of a living being really has an indeterminacy very similar to that of the concept 'language'" (*PG*, 192). Our ability to cope with such indeterminacy as it stands, without trying to fix sharp limits and thus to erase the indeterminacy, becomes a crucial theme in Wittgenstein's thought. You thus find him asking such questions as how many grains of sand make a heap (*PR*, 263)? How many angles must a polygon have before it looks like a circle (*PR*, 268)? How many houses does it take before a town begins to be a town (*PI*, §18)? In the same spirit, I also want to ask the following questions: How many words does a living being need to know before we could say that this living being possesses language? And where is exactly the dividing line between what is animated and what is inanimate, or between man and animal, or between a fetus and a human being, or a child and an adult? How can you clearly distinguish between people according to their race, sexuality, and so forth? Of course, a limit is drawn many times for special purposes. But can these limits abolish the indeterminacy that is inherent in life? And does a sharp limit have to be drawn in order for the concept of life to be used in a meaningful way? Wittgenstein replies: "Not at all!" (*PI*, §69). Which is not to say that language and life remain inexplicable or mysterious:

> Isn't flame mysterious because it is impalpable? All right—but why does that make it mysterious? Why should something impalpable be more mysterious than something palpable? Unless it's because we *want* to catch hold of it. (*Z*, §126)

The fact that concepts like language and life are impalpable (*ungreifbar*), the fact that they have vague boundaries, becomes a problem only if you *want* to catch hold of them by drawing sharp limits. But if you stand this temptation, this fantasy of circumscription, then you may no longer need to surrender to the *arcanum* of language and life.

4.5

Like the great fascination with the first words uttered by every child, it is interesting to look for the first words with which a thinker begins to articulate his or her own thought. In Wittgenstein's case, the first proposition of the *Tractatus*, signed in 1918, "The world is all that is the case" seems like the obvious candidate (*TLP*, §1). But I would like to suggest that the beginning of his philosophy is not this sweeping statement but an earlier claim from the very first entry in his philosophical notebooks dated from the summer of 1914: "Logic must take care of itself" (*NB*, 2). The problem, however, is that if this is how his philosophy *begins*, then this is also the way it must *end*: "How is it reconcilable with the task of philosophy," he continues by asking, "that logic should take care of itself?" (*ibid.*). If logic cares for itself, then why do we need philosophers to analyze the logical form of language? What, for example, is the value of analyzing propositions in the *Tractatus Logico-Philosophicus* in order to reach their elementary form? "Does such a complete analysis exist?"—he asks himself from the very start—"*And if not*: then what is the task of philosophy?!!?" (*ibid.*). It is intriguing to see how a very similar problem continues to occupy Wittgenstein's thought 20 years later. Again, we find him contemplating the dissolution of any general concept of language, which leads him to ask: "If the general concept of language dissolves in this way, doesn't philosophy dissolve as well?" (*PG*, 115). Only that now, in the mid-1930s, when his philosophical method is much more established than it was in 1914, Wittgenstein can offer us a definitive answer:

> No, for the task of philosophy is not to create a new, ideal language, but to clarify the use of our language, the existing language. Its aim is to remove particular misunderstandings; not to produce a real understanding for the first time. *(ibid.)*

In other words, there is really no "*great*, essential problem" behind our understanding of language, as there is also no great or essential problem at the bottom of our life (*PO*, 163). Of course, there are still endless problems, and philosophy can certainly help us to cope with them. Yes, Wittgenstein admits, "problems are solved (difficulties eliminated)," but "not a *single* problem" (*PI*, §133). This is the reason why the task of philosophy is not to imagine a new or ideal life but to clarify the living of our life, the existing life, by removing particular misunderstandings instead of achieving a complete understanding once and for all. As Wittgenstein does not want "to reform language," I am by no means asking here for the reformation of our form of life (*PI*, §132). From the *Tractatus'* insistence that "the propositions of our everyday language, just as they stand, are in perfect order" to the *Investigations'* persistence that "when I talk about language (words, sentences, etc.), I must speak the language of every day," it is clear that language, like life, with all their coarseness and materiality must take care of themselves (*TLP*, §5.5563; *PI*, §120). The attempt to put everything into its right place by mending this irreparable language and life is as hopeless as trying to "repair a torn spider's web with our fingers" (*PI*, §106).

When it comes to the task of philosophy, the basic intuition in the *Tractatus* proves to be very instructive when one comes to consider Wittgenstein's later writings. You can even read the *Tractatus* as a manifesto of the coming philosophy, and the later writings as an apprenticeship in this new vocation. As a whole, the way Wittgenstein imagines his philosophy of language can become an invaluable lesson for my attempt here to imagine a philosophy of life. "All philosophy," the *Tractatus* enounces, "is a 'critique of language'," as all philosophy could also be said to be a critique of life (*TLP*, §4.0031).

But instead of producing "philosophical propositions," the task of this critique is to bring about "clarifications" and "elucidations" of the way by which we speak and live (*TLP*, §4.112). This leads Wittgenstein to insist that, as we have seen, "philosophy is not a body of doctrine [*Lehre*] but an activity" (*ibid.*). The problem, however, is that since he declares in the Preface to the *Tractatus* that the book is not a *Lehrbuch* (a book of doctrine or a textbook), he cannot offer us particular instructions as to how the philosophical activity is to be practiced— how exactly are we supposed to be engaged in this critique, and how can we achieve clarifications and elucidations? It is obvious that the *Tractatus* is trying to bring about a kind of conversion of the reader. But since the fulfillment of the book is its transgression, it is also obvious that the *Tractatus* is at a loss when it comes to explaining the kind of activity that will take place if and when the ladder, this is to say, the book itself, is thrown away.

Even though the crystallization of Wittgenstein's later thought in *Philosophical Investigations* does not resemble a textbook at all, it can still be read as a series of "scenes of instruction" (Cavell 1990). In first sight, we may not feel that he is teaching us how to do philosophy, but after a little while we can certainly begin to see what it means to be engaged in a philosophical activity that is a continuous critique of language, which offers us neither a doctrine nor a thesis but numerous elucidations and clarifications. In virtually every remark of the *Investigations*, you can see Wittgenstein playing and even "struggling with language" (*CV*, 11). And this struggle or play is open ended— you never reach a stage in which you can claim that everything is quite easy now. There is no endgame when it comes to language-games. Because in actual language, as in actual life, "we make detours, we go by side-roads. We see the straight highway before us, but of course we cannot use it, because it is permanently closed" (*PI*, §426). In philosophy, every *cursus* is always an *excursus*. This, however, is not to say that the philosophical labor has no hope. Even though "there is not *a* philosophical method," the book shows us that "there are indeed methods, like different therapies," which we can practice in our continuous attempt to clarify the language that we speak or elucidate the life that we live (*PI*, §133). The labor of philosophy can still dissolve our problems "like a lump of sugar in water" and unravel, one by one, "the knots in our thinking," even though this labor "is as complicated as the knots that it unravels" (*PO*, 183).[37]

4.6

"Working in philosophy," Wittgenstein once wrote in his diary, "is really more a working on yourself" (*CV*, 16). This is essentially the reason why he is completely uninterested in making you accept a certain thesis or a doctrine or in leading you to believe that this and that is the case in the world or should be the case in the world. "I don't try to make you *believe* something you *don't* believe," he once told a student, "but to make you *do* something you won't do" (Rhees 1970: 43). This was an extremely important matter for Wittgenstein, who dreaded the moment his lifework would become the subject of lifeless works of philosophy. "I am by no means sure," he once commented, "that I should prefer a continuation of my work by others to a change in the way people live [*Lebensweise*], which would make all these questions superfluous" (*CV*, 61). So it seems that the only proper continuation of Wittgenstein's work is not a change in the way you think but in the way you live. After all, *doing* philosophy is always a matter of *undoing* philosophy, since "the real discovery is the one that makes me capable of stopping doing philosophy when I want to" (*PI*, §133). Philosophy is a therapy only if it is a therapy from philosophy itself. The essence of this therapy is not to see philosophy as a way of life but to see a way of life as philosophy:

> The sickness of a time is cured by an alteration in the mode of life [*Lebensweise*] of human beings, and it was possible for the sickness of philosophical problems to get cured only through a changed mode of thought and of life, not a medicine invented by an individual. (*RFM*, 57)[38]

Recall how I began this chapter by alluding to the metaphor of the ladder from the end of the *Tractatus*, where Wittgenstein writes: "My propositions serve as elucidations in the following way: anyone who understands me eventually recognizes them as nonsensical" (*TLP*, §6.54). In her analysis of this passage, Cora Diamond puts the emphasis on a single word: the word *me* (Diamond 2000: 150). She claims that Wittgenstein asks us to understand *him*, rather than to "understand" the "doctrine" of his nonsensical book. This insight, I believe, can be extended to the whole of Wittgenstein's work. Understanding *Wittgenstein*, in contrast to understanding *Wittgenstein's philosophy*, is not merely to understand a text but to understand a life. "Anyone who does not understand why we talk about these things must feel what we say to be mere trifling" (*Z*, §197). Anyone who does not understand that what needs to be grasped is not a body of writings but a form of life will continue to miss the point about Wittgenstein's thought. His work is not mere trifling. This philosophy, rather than being a "teaching which is not meant to apply to anything but the examples given," is a teaching "which '*points beyond*' them" (*PI*, §208). But again, this beyond is not an ineffable realm outside the reach of language, but the place in which language reaches out and touches life, the moment when a philosophy of language becomes a philosophy of life.

This is not to say, however, that there is a *particular* form of life that Wittgenstein asks you to grasp. As he says at the end of the Preface to the *Investigations*, "I should not like my writing to spare other people the trouble of thinking. But, if possible, to stimulate someone to thoughts of his own." In a similar vein, I could say that Wittgenstein's philosophy, or any philosophy whatsoever, should never spare you the trouble of living but, if possible, encourage you to examine, elucidate, and clarify your own life. Even in this present work of philosophy I am not really working on *Wittgenstein's* self but on *my* self. My task as a philosopher is not to submit to a form of life but to imagine a form of life, which may be part of the reason why Wittgenstein believed that "the philosopher is not a citizen of any community of ideas" (*Z*, §455). And so, my fellow philosophers, ask not what philosophy can do for you; ask what you can do for philosophy.

Chapter 5

Grammar

5.1

According to the *Tractatus*, "To give the essence of a proposition means to give the essence of all description, and thus the essence of the world" (*TLP*, §5.4711). But this clear-cut solution—give me the essence of language and I will give you the essence of the world—is rather misleading. A resolute reading of the *Tractatus* can only lead to the conclusion that the book is not meant to reveal to you a magical proposition that would express the essence of language and therefore lead you to discover the essence of the world. At most, it is set to show you that such an essence is a fiction. On the other hand, if you think that everything is quite easy now, if you are ready to conclude that the search for the incomparable essence of language is merely an illusion, then listen to what Wittgenstein has to say about this subject a decade after the completion of his *Tractatus*:

> What belongs to the essence of the world simply cannot be said. And philosophy, if it were to say anything, would have to describe the essence of the world. But the essence of language is a picture of the essence of the world; and philosophy as custodian [*Verwalterin*] of grammar can in fact grasp the essence of the world, only not in the propositions of language, but in rules for this language which exclude nonsensical combinations of signs. (*PR*, 85)

Here you can see how Wittgenstein's later, *grammatical* investigations is not going to simply abandon the search for essence—a search that began with his earlier, *logical* investigations. "We too in these investigations," he writes in the *Investigations*, "are trying to understand the essence of language—its function, its structure" (*PI*, §92). In another crucial remark from the same book, he states quite simply: "*Essence* is expressed by grammar" (*PI*, §371). Nevertheless, together with this important continuity in Wittgenstein's search for essence, there is a crucial discontinuity that must be emphasized: While logic is looking for a kind of essence that "lies *beneath* the surface . . . which an analysis digs out," grammar is searching for the essence that "already lies open to view" (*PI*, §92). Of course, changing *how* one is searching alters *what* one is searching for. As Wittgenstein presents the matter in his *Investigations*, it can be said that grammar is logic that lost its claim for "sublimity" or its "crystalline purity" (*PI*, §§89, 107). Although logic might suggest an "*ideal* language," and so it is "a logic for a vacuum," grammar functions within the fullness of *everyday* language (*PI*, §81). If a logician stands on "slippery ice," or "a ground without friction," then a grammarian walks on the "rough ground" of the concrete use of language (*PI*, §107). In short, grammar is logic that came back to its senses.

Looking at this development from the standpoint of his mature work, Wittgenstein describes logic as a "calculus according to definitive rules," which is "supposed to be something pure and clear-cut," something "*rigorous*" (*PI*, §§81, 105, 108). But this does not mean that a grammatical investigation is a logical investigation that has simply compromised its rigorousness. Wittgenstein admits in the *Investigations* that the "purity of logic" was not the *result* of his early work but its *requirement* (*PI*, §107). Now, he can remove this preconceived ideal, this pretense of purity, this insistence on sublimity, by rotating his whole investigation around, while keeping in place its axis—its real need to clarify the use of our words, which is the aim of all his investigations, whether they are labeled as "logical" or "grammatical." As Socrates believed that the unexamined life is not worth living, Wittgenstein's basic intuition is that the unexamined language is not worth speaking.

But what, precisely, does it entail to be a philosopher, this so to speak "custodian" of grammar? "The fundamental fact here," Wittgenstein explains, "is that we lay down rules . . . and that then when we follow the rules, things do not turn out as we had assumed. That we are therefore as it were entangled in our own rules" (*PI*, §125). As a consequence, what we "want to understand," what we need to "get a clear view of," is exactly this entanglement in our rules (*ibid.*). Because in the actual language of everyday life, in contrast to some dream of an ideal language, things do not always turn out as we had assumed, and so we find ourselves, time and again, entangled in the very rules that we wish to follow. Rules, we come to realize, can neither be imposed from above on the language that we speak nor can they ground it from below. Grammar is concerned with the intricate rules of the language that we already use in our complicated daily form of life. And this multiplicity of immanent rules, which sometimes unravel and sometimes untangle our lives, is what we want to understand, clarify, and elucidate.

In what follows, I will investigate this relationship between the rules of our language and the form of our life. "If I change the rules," Wittgenstein suggests, " . . . then I change the form, the meaning" (*PR*, 178). Rules, I will show, do not only reflect the meaning and the form of our language but also the meaning and the form of our lives. When you change the rules you do not only change what you say but also what you do and even what you are. This has to do with the fact that "the rule-governed nature of our language permeates our life" (*LWPPII*, 72). To imagine a form of life is to imagine the rules, or, one may say, *the grammar of life.* But there is another side to the same coin. It is only a life that has a form, a life that follows certain rules, which can function as the ground of our language: "It is characteristic of our language that the foundation on which it grows consists in steady ways of living [*Lebensformen*], regular ways of acting" (*PO*, 397). In other words, it is not only the understanding of rules that is necessary for our comprehension of lives. It is also impossible to grasp what Wittgenstein means by "following a rule" if you neglect life. Rush Rhees was the first to notice this negligence. He insists that one must "show how rules of grammar are rules of the lives in which there is language" (Rhees 1970: 45). In other words, if "language is part of an activity, or of a form of life," then the rules of language must also be, somehow, imbedded in our very lives (*PI*, §23).[39]

5.2

As Wittgenstein's later, grammatical, investigations revolve around the notion of rule, his earlier, logical, investigations are directed toward the concept of law. In a definitive formulation from the *Tractatus* we read: "The exploration of logic means the exploration of *everything that is subject to law.* And outside logic everything is accidental" (*TLP*, §6.3). Nevertheless, there is not one but three distinct kinds of laws in the *Tractatus*. The full manifestation of the force of law is to be found in the first type discussed in the book—logical laws—to which even God seems to be subjected: "It used to be said that God could create anything except what would be contrary to the laws of logic.—The truth is that we could not *say* what an 'illogical' world would look like" (*TLP*, §3.031). The only thing that can escape the force of logical laws are the laws of logic themselves: "Clearly the laws of logic cannot in their turn be subject to the laws of logic" (*TLP*, §6.123). But these exemplary laws soon give way to very different kinds of laws. Toward the end of the *Tractatus* we come to terms with the second type—the natural law—that appears to be less imposing than the logical one. In fact, Wittgenstein does not even take a natural law to be a law that nature is *subjected* to. Instead, it is seen as a kind of a matrix, like a pair of glasses, through which we *describe* the world around us. This pair of glasses can always be replaced by another pair, and it is only an "illusion" that natural laws can actually *explain* to us natural phenomena (*TLP*, §6.371). Philosophers of science can get really excited, or frustrated, by this idea. One thing, however, is quite clear: the force of natural laws is more tentative than the force of the formidable laws of logic. But everything becomes even more uncertain when, at the conclusion of the book, we arrive at the third type of laws of the ethical kind: "When an ethical law of the form, 'Thou shalt . . .' is laid down, one's first thought is, 'And what if I do not do it?'" (*TLP*, §6.422). The question, then, is how the subject of ethics, a human life, can be subjected to law? What is the force of a law that is neither logical nor natural but ethical? Remember, however, that Wittgenstein insists that *there can be no ethical propositions* (*TLP*, §6.42). Nevertheless, what if I, a living being, decide not to do what an ethical law—or, more correctly, what pretends to be an ethical law—tells me to? Could punishment or a certain intrinsic feeling of guilt simply do to make me correspond to this pseudo-law, to this illusion of an imperative, without any deviations? Put simply, our problem is the following: What is the relationship between law and life? The conclusion of Wittgenstein's *Tractatus* seems to indicate that the logical exploration to which the book is dedicated, this exploration into *everything that is subject to law*, cannot be applied to life without further complications.

In his later philosophy, Wittgenstein does not resolve the relationship between life and law by making this problem disappear. Instead, he presents a radically new way of thinking about this question by metamorphosing his early notion of law into his new concept of rule. His exploration of grammar, which is nothing but a rethinking of his earlier exploration of logic, may therefore be described as an exploration into the living beings that follow rules. Alternatively, one can say that grammar implies "that the forms I rely upon in making sense are human forms" (Cavell 1979: 29). In his later vision of language, those rules and those lives can hardly be thought of one without the other. Wittgenstein—who spent six years as an elementary school teacher after the completion of the *Tractatus*, during which he also published a small spelling dictionary for young students—saturates his later philosophy with scenes of instruction between students and teachers, children and adults. It is this passage from infancy to maturity, toward a life that is versed in the rules of a language and the form of a life, which his later philosophy seeks to illuminate.

"And what if I do not follow the rule?"—this question is not only sensible, but it must also always remain open. Nothing can force you to follow the rules that you tend to follow, the rules that guide whatever you say and do: not the threat of punishment in this world or the world hereafter, not an intrinsic feeling of guilt or sin, not a pragmatic or utilitarian calculation, not reason or explanation, and not coercion or compulsion. As Fernando Pessoa puts it, you need "to understand that grammar is an instrument, not a law" (Pessoa 1991: 13). It is you who use grammar, not the other way around. There can be no commandment that says, "Thou shalt play this language-game" or "Thou shalt partake in that form of life." If you follow certain rules, then you play a part in the community of those who also play the same language-game, who share the same form of life, who inhabit the same world that you inhabit. If you do not play according to certain rules (and you should not have the impression that there is something here that you must do or cannot do), then you simply do not communicate with those who do follow the rules; you lack this common ground with them, and you remain, to this particular extent, in a state of infancy. For those who do follow the rules, you are not in the wrong but in the dark; you are not mistaken but misguided. I cannot think of a better illustration of this state of infancy than the incident in which the daughter of Stanley Cavell smiled at a piece of fur, stroked it with her little hand, and called it "kitty." Her father explains:

> Kittens—what we call "kittens"—do not exist in her world yet, she has not acquired the forms of life which contain them. They do not exist in something like the way cities and mayors will not exist in her world until long after pumpkins and kittens do; or like the way God or love or responsibility or beauty do not exist in our world; we have not mastered, or we have forgotten, or we have distorted, or learned through fragmented models, the forms of life which could make utterances like "God exists" or "God is dead" or "I love you" or "I cannot do otherwise" or "Beauty is but the beginning of terror" bear all the weight they could carry, express all they could take from us. We do not know the meaning of the words. We look away and leap around. (Cavell 2000: 24)

But the fact that as we grow up we manage to move from infancy to maturity, that we learn to follow rules and speak meaningfully, is not to say that it is at all possible to somehow refine or reduce our language and life into an ultimate list of laws that applies to our multifarious language-games, to our complicated form of life. You must free yourself from the impression that somewhere, deep down or up high, there is a table of laws that you are unaware of, though you are still subjected to. "A law I'm unaware of isn't a law" (*PR*, 176). Remember: the essence of language is not hidden but lies open to view. As you can master the rules of a game simply by watching others play and then by partaking in this game, you can also master the rules that govern a language by attending to the way others speak and then following these rules as you use the language yourself. What guides your ability to follow a rule is not a theory but a practice. It is less a matter of knowledge and more of acknowledgment. Awareness to a rule is a kind of self-mastery: "To understand a sentence means to understand a language. To understand a language means to be master of a technique" (*PI*, §199). And in precisely the same way that the understanding of language is the mastery of a technique, understanding a form of life is simply the mastery of what the Greeks called a *techné tou biou*— a technique, or an art, of living. Despite our inclinations, we must realize that it is not a certain set of rules that masters a certain life; it is a certain life that masters a certain set of rules.[40]

5.3

In this intricate passage from infancy to maturity, "when we teach someone how to take his first step, we thereby enable him to go any distance" (*PR*, 200). But it also seems that the path we can take after the first step is somewhat decided by the teaching of a rule. When we follow a rule, do we simply choose how to follow it? There can certainly be something quite uncanny about the force of a rule:

> One does not feel that one has always got to wait upon the nod (whisper) of the rule. On the contrary, we are not on tenterhooks about what it will tell us next, but it always tells us the same, and we do what it tells us. (*PI*, §223)

Certain rules have a kind of a force that may therefore remind us the force of logical laws that we are familiar with from the *Tractatus*. Even though we are not "determined" by those rules "causally," Wittgenstein still seems to suggest that we are determined by them "logically" (*PI*, §220). We may thus definitely feel that some of our rules rule our lives. We tend to assume that the discipline of the rules that permeate our daily conduct "from within" is even more powerful than the command of any law that is imposed on life "from above." For instance, it is I, and no one else, who inflict upon myself those endless hours of writing and rewriting the lines that you are currently reading. So even though we do not necessarily think that our body is the prison of our soul, we still tend to believe that to some extent "the soul is the prison of the body," that the barrier to our actions lies within us (Foucault 1979: 30). We might therefore imagine that we cannot be otherwise than the way those inexplicable rules "tell" us to be. But this, if you follow Wittgenstein's analysis closely, is an illusion. It is an illusion of necessities and impossibilities that present the matter as if there is something that one cannot do or must do. From this perspective, the important thing is to realize that rules do not constitute the limits of our life; instead, they are our *limitations*.

The key for a more refined comprehension of the strange force of our rules is, again, the appeal to their place in our life: "Through custom," Wittgenstein states in a late manuscript, "these forms become a paradigm; they acquire so to speak the force of law" (*RPPI*, §343). For example, to say, "I am in pain" is a kind of a paradigm. This form of expression is such an inseparable element of our language, and our lives, that any attempt to doubt it is rather hopeless: "Could a legislator abolish the concept of pain? The basic concepts are interwoven so closely with what is most fundamental in our way of living [*Lebensweise*] that they are therefore unassailable" (*LWPPII*, 43–4). As long as a rule is closely interwoven within the fabric of life, as long as it is followed again and again, it possesses a certain paradigmatic force that no one, no matter how powerful, can refute. But when a rule is no longer a thread in the weave of life, when it is no longer followed, then its unassailable power simply fades into the air. We do not follow a rule because it has a force; a rule has a force because we follow it.

Since they always operate within the sphere of life, rules are far from being fixed forever. "If a pattern of life is the basis for the use of a word then the word must contain some amount of indefiniteness. The pattern of life, after all, is not one of exact regularity" (*LWPPI*, §211). The existence of some irregularity in our life is embodied in a language that its rules have a certain level of flexibility: "For in the flux of life, where all our concepts are elastic, we couldn't reconcile ourselves to a rigid concept" (*LWPPI*, §246). As a result, Wittgenstein's later philosophy rises and falls on its ability to imagine a language and a form of life that are somewhat hazy and indeterminate, rather than simply clear and distinct: "The greatest difficulty in these investigations," he writes in one of his last notebooks, "is to find a way to represent vagueness" (*LWPPI*, §347). In other words, he must account not only for the moments in which we follow our rules rather blindly and everything works according to plan but also for this ubiquitous grey zone in which things do not turn out as we had assumed, when we find ourselves entangled in our own rules:

> If a concept depends on a pattern of life, then there must be some indefiniteness in it. For if a pattern deviates from the norm, what we want to say here would become quite dubious. Thus can there be definiteness only where life flows quite regularly? But what do they do when they come across an irregular case? Maybe they just shrug their shoulders. (*RPPII*, §652–3)

When it comes to a life that stops flowing regularly, when its pattern deviates from the norm, Wittgenstein cannot act like those unspecified "they" from the quote above. In the role of a custodian of grammar, he cannot simply shrug his shoulders. He must investigate not only the rule but also the exception to the rule.

As we have seen, the early Wittgenstein claims that within the laws of logic *nothing* is accidental, while outside their jurisdiction *everything* is accidental. Rules, on the other hand, do not have the privilege of such clear distinction between an inside and an outside, lawfulness and lawlessness. They must have a level of elasticity by allowing deviations or exceptions. If "our rules leave loop-holes open," then "the practice has to speak for itself" (*OC*, §139). When such a loop-hole appears, you cannot rely on the rule as if it was a user manual for life. You will wait in vain for the nod or the whisper of the rule to tell you what to do. At a moment of uncertainty, all your idle talk and mechanical activity must give way to thought. At a moment of exception, when many things seem accidental, when many things seem possible, you cannot overestimate the importance of your personal judgments and singular deeds. Here, life becomes interesting.[41]

Because unlike a law, a rule is only an approximation—it applies only *most* of the times: "If I state 'That's the rule,' that only has a sense as long as I have determined the maximum number of exceptions I'll allow before knocking down the rule" (*PR*, 293). Consider this simple (or simplistic) example: You learn in life to trust your senses (a rule), even though you also learn that in special cases you cannot trust them (an exception). But do you have a determinate number of exceptions, when you are being deceived, which you will allow before knocking down the rule and stop trusting your senses altogether? We need to distinguish, therefore, "between a mistake for which, as it were, a place is prepared in the game, and a complete irregularity that happens as an exception" (*OC*, §647). What would happen, then, if the normal state of rule transformed into a total state of exception?

> If things were quite different from what they actually are—if there were for instance no characteristic expression of pain, or fear, or joy; if rule became exception and exception a rule; or if both became phenomena of roughly equal frequency—this would make our normal language-games lose their point. (*PI*, §142)

In this zone of complete indetermination, where the rule and the exception cannot be distinguished from one another, the representation of vagueness transforms into the threat of arbitrariness, and the potentiality of infancy becomes the actuality of anarchy. In order to avoid this predicament, the exception, though it can and should never be abolished, must have a delimited place in our language and our life. We always need to maintain a delicate *im*balance between the rule and the exception. Otherwise, if the rule becomes the exception and the exception becomes the rule, then we reach a point where, indeed, everything is accidental, everything is possible, and the fabric of our language-games and our forms of life unravels into meaningless strands.

5.4

How, then, do we maintain this precarious fabric of rules that are woven into language and life? How, despite their vagueness and elasticity, are we still able to determine whether rules are followed correctly or incorrectly? Is there some sort of an invisible hand that regulates the application of our rules? Do we have some inner conscience that directs our conduct? Think, once again, about the rules of a game. Even though you do not always consult a written list of rules as you play, and even though there is not necessarily a referee who decides in each moment whether or not you are playing correctly, you can still play according to certain rules without giving the matter a second thought. "Smith and Brown play chess with no difficulty. Do they understand the game? Well, they play it. And they understand the rules in the sense of following them" (*PO*, 367). In Rush Rhees' notes from one of Wittgenstein's lectures, from which the last quote is extracted, I also found a curious exchange about this seemingly unproblematic issue, which may have taken place between Wittgenstein and a student, or, more likely, between Wittgenstein and himself: "How do we control the game?—By the rules.—But do we control the application of the rules?—No.—What then does it mean to control by the rules?—Just that people do in fact act in certain ways" (*PO*, 352). But the question remains unanswered: How do we decide whether people who are acting in certain ways are following the rules rightly or wrongly? Is it enough that each player simply *believes* that he or she is following the rules as they should be followed? But "doesn't this lead to anarchy?"—we hear the question asked, to which Wittgenstein replies: "No, for the police ((law enforcement)) which stops the anarchy acts in the public language" (*ibid.*). What, then, is this "language police" that is dedicated to the "enforcement" of the law and the protection from the threat of anarchy? Is this what it means to be a philosopher, this "custodian" of grammar?

The rejection of such an interpretation lies in the end of the quote above: "for the police ((law enforcement)) which stops the anarchy *acts in the public language*." We do not follow rules because we fear some sort of a special clandestine police that monitors language from above or from below by enforcing its laws, but simply because language is *public*. Anarchy, like its enforcement, does not exist in a sort of a state of exception. Exceptions do not exist *outside* our language-games and forms of life; they are an absolutely integral part of them. They always exist in an intimate relation to a shared set of rules, a shared way of acting, and a shared way of living. Without a language that is public we could have no criteria to decide whether a rule is followed rightly or wrongly, and we would not be able to direct its application. As a result, the question which the whole discussion about rules is directed toward is the following: "Is what we call "obeying a rule" something that it would be possible for only *one* man to do, and to do only *once* in his life?" (*PI*, §199). And if this makes no sense, then what does it say about the very idea of following a rule? For instance, can you simply *know* the correct application of a rule? "But what does this knowledge consist in? Let me ask: *when* do you know that application? Always? Day and night? Or only when you are actually thinking of the rule?" (*PI*, §148). And even if you are thinking about the application of the rule at this very moment, does it necessarily entail that you actually know how to follow it in real life? Remember: "Obeying a rule is a practice. And to *think* one is obeying a rule is not to obey a rule," which leads Wittgenstein to make the decisive statement that stands behind all these considerations: "Hence it is not possible to obey a rule 'privately': otherwise thinking one was obeying a rule would be the same thing as obeying it" (*PI*, §202).

To say that a rule cannot be followed privately is not to say that I cannot learn a rule and then follow it correctly on my own without the scrutiny of others. Robinson Crusoe, for example, continues on his deserted island to follow the meticulous rules that permeated the life of every Englishman. After he learned to master these rules back at home, he was able to go on and apply them without the need of other Englishmen to approve or disprove of his actions on the island. But Wittgenstein's point is different. In the beginning of his own notes for one of his lectures from the mid-1930s, you find this unexplained side-remark: "The Diary of Robinson Cr" (*PO*, 447). Its elucidation can be found elsewhere:

> Robinson Crusoe may have held soliloquies. And then he talks to himself alone. But he talks the language he has talked with people before. But imagine him inventing a *private* language. Imagine that he gives a name to a sensation of his. What then does he do with it?— Suppose he kept a diary, and that in this diary he put x against each day when he had a toothache. (*PO*, 320)

"The diary of Robinson Crusoe" is what became in the *Investigations* the prime example for the "private language argument," as scholars tend to call it. The "argument" goes something like this: if you keep a diary in which you write a certain sign every time you have a certain feeling, then how are you going to assure yourself, or others, that you really have the same feeling every time you write the same sign? What is the criterion for the correctness or incorrectness of the rule that you believe that you established for yourself (every time I feel this feeling I write this sign)? So you are led to realize that the "private rule" that you thought that you possess is actually only the illusion of a rule: "I want to play chess, and a man gives the white king a paper crown, leaving the use of the piece unaltered, but telling me that the crown has a meaning to him in the game, which he can't express by rules"— to which Wittgenstein replies: "As long as it doesn't alter the use of the piece, it hasn't what I call a meaning" (*BB*, 65). To say that only I know how to follow my own rule because only I know what my words stand for turns out to be not exactly wrong but simply nonsensical. It is like saying that only I know how tall I am, and then, in order to prove it, I put my hand on top of my head (*PI*, §279).

But the "private language argument"—which may seem tedious, obscure, or simply strange and is perhaps the single most controversial moment in Wittgenstein's *Investigations*—is never presented by the author of the book as an "argument" for the promotion of the "thesis" that there is no private language. I think that one of the sources of this confusion is the isolation of the "private language argument" from its context. The remarks of the *Investigations* may indeed be likened to pictures in an album. But you must bear in mind that these remarks also function as the parts of a complicated philosophical machine: "I set the brake up by connecting up rod and lever," we hear one voice in the beginning of the book, to which a second voice replies: "Yes, given the whole of the rest of the mechanism. Only in conjunction with that is it a brake-lever, and separated from its support it is not even a lever; it may be anything, or nothing" (*PI*, §6). Without the whole philosophical mechanism of the *Investigations*, the "private language argument" may be anything, or nothing. Let us, then, take a closer look at the machine in which this "argument" finds its support.

Saul Kripke was the first to show that the discussion of rules is the background to the problem of private language (Kripke 1982). Yet he still fails to fully appreciate the importance of a crucial remark that Wittgenstein uses as a sort of key that opens the door to this formidable problem. Immediately before the "argument" begins, we hear the imaginary interlocutor ask "So you are saying that human agreement decides what is true and what is false?", to which Wittgenstein replies "It is what human beings *say* that is true and false; and they agree in the *language* they use. That is not agreement in opinions, but in form of life" (*PI*, §241). I believe that Wittgenstein's vision of an agreement in the language human beings use, this agreement in form of life, is the background that renders the idea of a private language so absurd. The point of this "argument," Cavell explains, "is to release the fantasy expressed in the denial that language is something essentially shared" (Cavell 1979: 344). An agreement in form of life is not a contract, and following rules cannot be a matter of enforcement. It is only in virtue of our shared existence that rules can have followers, and life can become agreeable.[42]

5.5

In order to better understand what the mechanism of Wittgenstein's philosophy is set to achieve, you also need to examine the remarks that come immediately after the "private language argument," where he raises one of the truly disquieting questions that his *Investigations* poses to thought (as if the "private language argument" was a strategic move meant to distract the reader from the truly radical moment): What is the importance of our inner experiences to the way we use language? If it is only an illusion that a private experience could guarantee that a word is used according to a certain rule, then what is the place of this private experience in our public discourse? If language is no longer seen as a simple mirror of the external world, could it still be conceived as a reflection of an inner life? Can internal thoughts constitute the meaning of external words? Or is it possible to transform the agreement of a word with an inner state to a state of agreement in form of life? Here we can detect "a radical break with the idea that language always functions in one way, always serves the same purpose: to convey thoughts—which may be about houses, pains, good and evil, or anything else you please" (*PI*, §304). As a result, Wittgenstein can no longer take for granted the idea that words reveal what is hidden or that actions make public what is private:

> There is a kind of general disease of thinking which always looks for (and finds) what would be called a mental state from which all our acts spring as from a reservoir. Thus one says, "The fashion changes because the taste of people changes." The taste is the mental reservoir. But if a tailor today designs a cut of dress different from that which he designed a year ago, can't what is called his change of taste have consisted, partly or wholly, in doing just this? (*BB*, 143)

The belief that my existence—what I says and what I do—is the external manifestation of my concealed essence, the view that a living being is a fountainhead of a "mental reservoir," is the disease of thought that Wittgenstein hopes to cure us from. He considers the notion of "private experience" to be a "degenerated construction of our grammar," or a "grammatical monster," which constantly fools us; however, "when we wish to do away with it, it seems as though we denied the existence of experience, say, toothache" (*PO*, 283). Wittgenstein, it is important to note, does not try to deny anything. He does not want to promote the thesis that there is no private experience or no inner life. In fact, he declares early on: "The distinction between 'inner' and 'outer' does not interest us" (*PG*, 100). He does not try to renounce the existence of those grammatical monsters, but to show that they are only shadows on the bedroom's wall, by awakening us from the daydream in which we take the private chambers of our soul to explain the way we speak or the way we live. He helps us see that we could come to terms with the grammar of our language, and the grammar of our life, without reverting to some kind of a shadowy internal grammar.

This brings me to my main question: What, at the end of the day, is a *private life*? Is it the life that is lived in the sanctuary of one's home? To the extent that you share your home with others, even if they are family, friends, or lovers, this life is not, properly speaking, private. If you live a life that others cannot see and scrutinize, like a life on a deserted island or in a closed room, but you continue to do the things that you used to do when others were around, then this is also not exactly a private life. Nevertheless, these two scenarios are what we usually have in mind when we think about a "private life," even though we know from our own experience that such a life is in fact extremely codified by rules that are far from being our own private inventions. So let me press the question one more time: can you live a life that only you can experience and only you can understand? Can you live a life according to your own private rules that you invented, which only you bother to follow on a regular basis, according to your own discretion? *Can you imagine a private form of life?* Think again about the diary of Robinson Crusoe. An interesting point about this example that seems to evade the scrutiny of many commentators is that the practice of *keeping a diary* and the practice of *writing a sign that stands for a feeling* are not private inventions at all, but a part of an activity, or of a form of life, which many of us share and all of us can follow. Remember the importance of showing how a rule of grammar is a rule of the lives in which there is language. Even in Wittgenstein's attempt to imagine a private language with a private rule, he still fails to imagine a private form of life. You can *try* to imagine a truly private form of life, but it will eventually lead you to an absurdity, or nonsensicality, which would then dissolve this "thing" that you wished to imagine.[43]

"What gives the impression," Wittgenstein asks, "that we want to deny anything," like the existence of an "inner process" (*PI*, §305)? In this context, I would like to maintain that, first and foremost, I do not want to give the impression that I wish to deny, in the midst of this shared life, a place for the singular or the personal. After all, there is no uniform way by which one could appropriate a form of life in order to call it one's own. You still have a personal responsibility in the conduct of everyday life, even if you feel alienated from the form of life in which you happen to partake. But I do want to insist that the significance of singularity or personality lies in its ability to make itself manifest, that it is not merely a hidden private affair. Once again, the point is not the disappearance of the inner or the private, but *the disappearance of the temptation to make a simplistic separation between the inner and the outer, the private and the public, the singular and the common, the personal and the political.* What we want to do away with is this metaphysical idea that the way we live emanates from some sort of a hidden reservoir, that our private life constitutes our form of life. In this spirit, instead of thinking about the eye as the window of the soul, try to imagine, together with Wittgenstein, that "the face is the soul of the body" (*CV*, 23).

And these are, of course, comments about the *grammar* of the word "life." Life, as this term is used here, is understood as a form of life. This form is not *added* to a life. Life *is* always already a form of life. And since we need to have a certain level of agreement in form of life, this agreement, and this form, is never one's private brainchild. So even though Aristotle takes humans to be the living beings that have language, it is crucial to realize that we do not "have" language in the sense of "having" private property, like a car or a house. Remember that language, like happiness, is a form of activity, and an activity is something that comes into being and not something that you can possess all the time.[44] Wittgenstein thus reminds us "that *words* are public property" (*PO*, 406). A language-game and a form of life can have no owner. If we take "the world" to be a sort of a shared public space, or even as "a space for politics," then a form of life, as I imagine it, is always already a life that is lived within this world; a life that is, so to speak, "thrown" into this shared world in such a way that the world and life can be said to be one (Arendt 2000: 17).

5.6

This point may become a bit clearer if we reexamine Wittgenstein's pivotal claim that "to imagine a language means to imagine a form of life" (*PI*, §19). I would like to suggest that *vorstellen*, which is translated here as "to imagine," is more than a mere act of our inner imagination. *Vorstellen* also means "to present"—to place before, put in front of, or put forward. We may therefore render the whole sentence as follows: "To present a language means to present a form of life." Language and life do not *represent* (*darstellen*) something, as a picture represents a fact.[45] A language-game does not mirror the inner life or the external world. A form of life is not a reflection of what lies deep down or up high. By speaking, you simply place before others a language-game. By living, you put in front of you a form of life. You do not represent your rules and you do not exactly comply with them either, because you *are* the rules; the rules are your form of life. By living, you therefore present these rules to others, with the hope of achieving an agreement in form of life. And even though "here one is tempted again and again to talk more than still makes sense," "to continue talking where one should stop," Wittgenstein knows that the explanation of a rule "can only be shown by *example*" (*RPPII*, §41–2). We teach by setting an example, by presenting our form of life. Leo Tolstoy elucidates this matter beautifully in *Gospel in Brief*, a book about which Wittgenstein once said that it "virtually kept me alive" (*WSP*, 91). Tolstoy writes:

> For when one lights a candle, one does not put it under a bench, but on the table, that it may light all in the room. So, you also, do not hide your light, but show it by your works, so that men may see that you know the truth. (Tolstoy 1997: 73)[46]

Chapter 6

Certainty

6.1

You present your form of life through your words and your deeds. Another person bears witness to the way you live your life. But what will it take for the other to see what you wish to show? How do the both of you come to agree on the language that you use? And how do you achieve an agreement in form of life? In a remark from the early 1930s, Wittgenstein writes: "To convince someone of the truth, it is not enough to state it, but rather one must find the *path* from error to truth" (*PO*, 119). What, then, constitutes this murky path leading from error to truth?

Imagine a drawing of an old man walking up a steep path leaning on a stick. Wittgenstein questions our perception of such a picture with a rather wicked suggestion: "Might it not have looked just the same if he had been sliding downhill in that position? Perhaps a Martian would describe the picture so. I do not need to explain why *we* do not describe it so" (*PI*, 54). You may wonder why is Wittgenstein so cold toward the bewildered Martian? Isn't it still possible to offer various explanations that will guide the alien on the path from error to truth? But in what sense could the way *we* describe the picture be said to be "the truth"? And who are those "we" Wittgenstein speaks about?

Living beings may look at things, say things, believe in things, and do things very differently from one another. What this could suggest is that "there is an enormous gulf between us" (*LC*, 58). When Wittgenstein confronts this enormous gulf between the Martian and himself, he has no pretensions that he could erase it by means of simple explanations or even elaborate ones. He cannot enforce an agreement in form of life. Of course, this is not only true about the difference between humans and aliens. Many times, "one human being can be a complete enigma to another" (*PI*, 223). If this is indeed the case, you might be tempted to offer reasons and explanations as to why you live your life the way you do. But what if your explanations fall on deaf ears, and your reasons just lead to more questions? What if the complete enigma, the enormous gulf, persists? In such a case, Wittgenstein suggests, "it would now be no use to say: 'But can't you see . . . ?'—and repeat the old examples and explanations" (*PI*, §185). From the first remark of *Philosophical Investigations*, his reaction to one's temptation to offer more and more reasons is simple and unequivocal: "Explanations come to an end somewhere" (*PI*, §1). There are times, he insists, when the best reply to repeated questions about the way we speak, or the way we live, may not be further explanations. In a definitive formulation, he states: "If I have exhausted my justifications I have reached bedrock, and my spade is turned. Then I am inclined to say: 'This is simply what I do'" (*PI*, §217).

Notice, however, that "This is simply what I do" is not the only possible response to the repeated questions of the inquisitive Martian. One may also be inclined to state in such a situation something like, "This is how things stand" or "This is how it has to be!" Imagine two characters, call them C and K, who stand in front of the puzzled visitor from outer space. To the repeated questions of the alien, K finally says: "This is how it has to be," while C replies: "This is simply what I do." So what is really the difference between K and C's responses? I think that when K insists, "This is how it has to be," he tries to *force* the Martian to accept his form of life. But when C answers, "This is simply what I do," then it is C, and not the alien, who is forced to reach a state of acceptance. "My *life*," Wittgenstein writes, "consists in my being content to accept many things" (*OC*, §344). After C exhausted his justifications and he says, "This is simply what I do," he does not try to impose or enforce an agreement in form of life. He no longer attempts to convince—neither the Martian, nor himself— of the validity of his conduct. He simply wishes to present an aspect of his form of life to the Martian. He teaches by giving a description, not by giving an explanation, with the hope that the alien is in a position to see what is shown to him. "Here," Wittgenstein suggests, "one can only *describe* and say: this is what human life is like" (*PO*, 121). For Stanley Cavell, this moment is the quintessence of Wittgenstein's philosophy: "That the justifications and explanations we give of our language and conduct, that our ways of trying to intellectualize our lives, do not really satisfy us, is what, as I read him, Wittgenstein wishes us above all to grasp" (Cavell 2000: 26).[47]

Confronting this inability to fully justify and explain neither language nor life might lead you to be skeptical about the language that you speak and doubt this whole life that you live, since nothing that you say or do can be firmly grounded. But you also need to realize that "doubting," exactly like reasoning, "has to come to an end somewhere" (*PO*, 377). When you come to think about it, "a doubt without an end is not even a doubt," but a sort of a "hollow" doubt (*OC*, §§312, 625). As we have seen, any doubt must be, "*essentially*, an exception to the rule," since it has to find its place within the "environment" of the rule (*PO*, 379). For example, a game does not *begin* when the players doubt its rules. Doubt may appear only after the environment of the rules of the game has been established. Accordingly, Wittgenstein can claim that "the primitive form of the language-game is certainty, not uncertainty. For uncertainty could never lead to action" (*PO*, 397). In this way, alongside a skeptical attitude of doubt, Wittgenstein promotes what I take to be his gesture of acceptance. The sense of deep separation between living beings cannot be the end of the story (nor its beginning), because Wittgenstein is also very attentive to the fact that we may see things, say things, believe in things, and do things in a similar way to one another. Our different modes of living might also be different modifications of the same life. After all, we *do* share a form of life, have a common language, and even hold on to the same truth. When Wittgenstein uses the pronoun "we" he means nothing more, but nothing less, than this. The enormous gulf between us can very easily transform into a simple touch. And this is what, as I read him, Wittgenstein wants us above all to grasp.

6.2

But what is it, exactly, that you need to accept? When Wittgenstein claims that his *life* consists in his being content to accept many things, what are those "many things" that he learns to accept? The answer is that what you are always content to accept in your life are *forms* of life: "What has to be accepted, the given, is—so one could say—*forms of life*" (*PI*, 226). One way of approaching this crucial remark is to say that, in the spirit of the *Tractatus*, where Wittgenstein observes how "people today stop at the laws of nature, treating them as something inviolable, just as God and Fate were treated in past ages," the *Investigations* seems to consider neither natural laws, nor God, nor Fate, but *forms of life*, as this sort of "a clear and acknowledged *terminus*" (*TLP*, §6.372). Though I am far from claiming that forms of life are inviolable, I still want to insist that one can challenge their legitimacy only because others accept them as a given. You simply cannot imagine a form of life without some level of acceptance. You pass over a form of life in silence—not because a form of life is *something* that exists beyond the reach of language, but because there is simply nothing to explain, because any "explanation" of a form of life is revealed, sooner or later, as plain nonsense. This thing that we want to grasp always slips through our fingers. A form of life is therefore a *terminus* not in the sense of a limit but in the sense of a limitation. When it comes to a form of life, I must realize that any attempt to ground this activity will eventually come to an end. I must be aware that "my reasons will soon give out. And then I shall act, without reasons" (*PI*, §211). A form of life is simply what I do, or better, it is what *we* do. It is what we agree upon when we have this "we." It is what we accept when we share a community. It is what we take as the given when we converse with each other, or live with each other, which in Wittgenstein's philosophy comes to the same thing (as the etymology of "conversation" from "living together," shows). In a form of life, living is always already a living-with, in such a way that any limitation is also the liberation from one's own sense of separation.

It is worth mentioning that there is another version of the remark about "what has to be accepted . . ." in Wittgenstein's manuscripts. It begins with the observation "that we act in such-and-such ways, e.g. *punish* certain actions, *establish* the state of affair thus and so, *give* orders, render accounts, describe colors, take an interest in others' feelings," which then leads him to state: "What has to be accepted, the given—it might be said—are facts of living" (*RPPI*, §630). Again, it will be interesting to contrast this variation with the early philosophy. Here we could see how *facts*, which were the building blocks of the world at the time of the *Tractatus* ("The world is the totality of facts"; "The world divides into facts"), transform in this late manuscript to "facts of living" (*TLP*, §§1.1, 1.2). These "facts of living" cannot simply be objective facts in the external world, since they are virtually "fused into the foundations of our language-game" (*OC*, §558). They are imbedded in our form of life. This leads Wittgenstein to insist time after time that it is always within the realm of *my life* that I come to consider particular facts as given or as certain: "*My life* shows that I know or am certain that there is a chair over there, or a door, and so on" (*OC*, §7, emphasis added). And again: "Now do I, in the course of *my life*, make sure I know that here is a hand—my own hand, that is?" (*OC*, §9, emphasis added). And again:

> Why is it not possible for me to doubt that I have never been on the moon? And how could I try to doubt it? First and foremost, the supposition that perhaps I have been there would strike me as *idle*. Nothing would follow from it, nothing be explained by it. It would not tie in with anything in *my life*. (*OC*, §117, second emphasis added)

Within a form of life there is an intricate network of multiple facts of living, which come together to form a sort of a system, and this system is what we accept as we go about living our lives. Wittgenstein, however, insists that "this system is not a more or less arbitrary and doubtful point of departure for all our arguments . . . as [it is] the element in which arguments have their life [since this system is their *Lebenselement*]" (*OC*, §105). Which is not to say that such a system is an arbitrary ground that we can use in order to explain, prove, test, confirm, or disconfirm whatever we say or do. A form of life is not an axiom of life. If we take whatever we argue for and strip it of its environment, of the system that we call a form of life, then our argument is not groundless, but nonsense or lifeless—it loses its "living element." A form of life may therefore be understood not as the foundation at the bottom of our thought, but as "the scaffolding of our thought," which must support it from all sides (*OC*, §211). It is never a single thing that we consider as the ground but always a whole cluster of elements which depend on each other and come together in order to create this elaborate scaffolding of language and life. In short, "what I hold fast to is not *one* proposition but a nest of propositions" (*OC*, §225). Imagine for a moment that humans are birds, and their propositions are the twigs that they gather together in order to build a nest. Alternatively, think about life as a "weave" with multiple "patterns," which are closely knit together in order to create the fabric of our existence (*LWPPII*, 42). These metaphors of the scaffolding, the nest, and the fabric may help you to accept that which has to be accepted, and bring you closer to an understanding of what Wittgenstein means when he speaks about "forms of life."

I tend to accept many things not because I am unable to doubt them, but because these things function like the hinges of a door, and "if I want the door to turn, the hinges must stay put" (*OC*, §343). Wittgenstein calls these hinges, these things that have to be accepted, *paradigms*: "What looks as if it *had* to exist, is part of the language. It is a paradigm in our language-game; something with which comparison is made" (*PI*, §50). What, then, is a paradigm? A paradigm is something about which we are tempted to say, "This is how it has to be," because a paradigm gives the impression that it *had* to exist. But in fact, the proper reaction to a paradigm is to say, again, "This is simply what I do." Let me try to explain this point. What looks as if it had to exist is simply a part of the life that I live. Of course, *what I do*, how I live my life, what I feel certain about, is not a *necessity*, which others *must* comply with, but a *possibility*, which others *can* use as they make comparisons with their own lives. Even though what I do is only what *I* do, I still present this life as a paradigm for other living beings. Even if I am uncertain about something, I still *present* this uncertainty so others may compare it with their own sense of certainty. Other times, "I act with *complete* certainty. But this certainty is my own" (*OC*, §174). Seeing a form of life as a paradigm therefore allows us to have a kind of certainty that is not reduced to a dogma. A paradigm enables us to treat our lives as a power that is not a coercive one—to live and let live.

Take a move of a piece in a board game as a first example. Wittgenstein explains that "moving a piece could be conceived in these two ways: as a paradigm for future moves, or as a move in an actual game," and so "in one case we make a move in an existent game, in the other we establish a rule of the game" (Z, §294). The paradigm of a game, one may say, is simply to play the game. Other people, who bear witness to the way you play, can use your moves as an example for the way they should play as well. From this perspective, it can be said that anything that you say may be conceived not only as a move in an actual language-game but also as a paradigm for future moves in a language-game. And when I live my life, I am not only moving within an established form of life, because I may also be establishing, by means of my actions, a new rule of a form of life. By living, we sometimes *play* with a form of life, and this play can transform an existing form.

Now consider a second example: the practice of literary citation. The moment a written text is cited in another text, the first text becomes a sort of a paradigm in the context of the second text. For instance, when I quote here, time and again, Wittgenstein's words, I do not take what he says to be a proof for what I want to say, nor do I consider what I say as an attempt to prove what he wants to say. Instead, I consider these quotes as paradigms—I take his words as objects of comparison with my own words. Now, what I am trying to say here is that any moment in our lives may be, so to speak, cited within the context of another life. Anything that we say has the poten- tiality of becoming an object of comparison. Everything that we do can become a hinge on which another life turns. And as every life can be cited within another life, every life is full to the brim with citations from a multiplicity of lives. This is not to say, however, that whatever you say, or whatever you do, does not really matter, since everything in life could also be otherwise than the way it is, because it is all just a citation of a citation of a citation. Instead, I think that Wittgenstein leads you to the exact opposite conclusion: Whatever you say and do matters. Everything can become a "*citation à l'ordre du jour*" (Benjamin 1968: 254). So instead of promoting a skeptical attitude toward an existent form of life, instead of negating a form of life, you are urged to affirm a form of life—not by explaining it but simply by living it; not by saying but through showing (as the etymology of "paradigm," "to show itself besides," indicates). To live, in this sense, is to perform a form of life.

6.3

Consider now the last time in which Wittgenstein uses the term "form of life" in his writings. The occasion is his final remarks on the subject of certainty. He begins by distinguishing between two modes of certainty: a "comfortable" certainty and a certainty that is still "struggling" (*OC*, §357). A comfortable certainty can be best exemplified in the statement, "This is simply what I do," while a good manifestation of a struggling certainty is the assertion, "This is how it has to be." "Now," Wittgenstein writes, "I would like to regard this [comfortable] certainty, not as something akin to hastiness or superficiality, but as a form of life. (That is very badly expressed and probably badly thought as well)" (*OC*, §358). His dissatisfaction with this first formulation immediately leads to its modification: "But that means I want to conceive it as something that lies beyond being justified or unjustified; as it were, as something animal [*animalisches*]" (*OC*, §359). Notice how Wittgenstein shifts from regarding certainty as a form of life to regarding this certainty as something animalistic. Like his alternation between "facts of living" and "forms of life," this turn in phrasing is very decisive. It can show you that, in opposition to traditional thought that insists on the separation of "man" and "animal," "form of life" and "fact of life," in Wittgenstein's philosophy these dualisms make little or simply no sense:

> I want to regard man here as an animal; as a primitive being to which one grants instincts but not ratiocination [*Raisonnement*]. As a creature in a primitive state. Any logic good enough for a primitive means of communication needs no apologies from us. Language did not emerge from some kind of ratiocination. (*OC*, §475)

But I think that it will be a mistake to assume that Wittgenstein is hinting in these Nietzschian remarks at the possibility of *reducing* man to an animal, form of life to fact of life, reason to instinct. I want to claim that what he is trying to do here is to *question* the clear-cut barrier that exists between these two realms from time immemorial. Remember the Aristotelian tendency to consider man to be a sort of living being with the additional capacity to use language. Over time, this basic intuition developed a life of its own, to the point in which it seems that without language there is no man but only an animal, no form of life but only the fact of being alive. But what Wittgenstein helps us to see is that language, instead of being the thing that separates the first from the second, could be precisely what brings them together:

> It is sometimes said that animals do not talk because they lack the mental capacity. And this means: "they do not think, and that is why they do not talk." But—they simply do not talk. Or to put it better: they do not use language—if we except the most primitive forms of language.—Commanding, questioning, recounting, chatting, are as much a part of our natural history as walking, eating, drinking, playing. (*PI*, §25)

Speaking is an inseparable part of our living, like walking, eating, drinking, playing, etc. I speak—"this is simply what I do." But why do you think that this is "how it has to be?" Remember that speaking is not the whole activity but only a part of an activity. Language cannot *define* this activity or this human form of life. The possession of language is by no means the *ground* of our lives. To say that my language is inseparable from my living is not to make a metaphysical claim about the essence of man. At most, it is simply to say that speaking is a part of my nature as much as it is a part of my history, or my culture. After all, our rational history is just another chapter in the book of our natural history. This is perhaps what makes from the certainty that I have as a speaking living being into a comfortable certainty, rather than a struggling one. And maybe because speaking is a part of my "comfort zone," I can also bring myself to keep silent when there is nothing to say.

The centrality of language to the human form of life should therefore not blind you to Wittgenstein's basic realization that "Language . . . is a refinement, 'in the beginning was the deed'" (*CV*, 31). Here, as in a few other places in his writings, we find this quote from Goethe's *Faust*, "*Im Anfang war die Tat*," "In the beginning was the deed," as an alternative to the opening verse in Saint John's Gospel, "In the beginning was the Word." Wittgenstein even contemplated using Goethe's sentence as the motto for his philosophical project. Once again, through this simple substitution of "deed" for "word," you come to see that words do not come before deeds, that words are not separate from deeds. For Wittgenstein, there is in fact no simple distinction between the two, partly because, as we have seen, "words are also deeds" (*PI*, §546). This is to show that the philosopher who is usually credited as the messiah of the linguistic turn never really claims that there is any primacy to language. If you insist to search for what lies "in the beginning," then you will find that a word in language is indistinguishable from a deed in life; then you will see that in the word was life.

Ten days before his death, Wittgenstein writes: "You must bear in mind that the language-game is so to say something unpredictable. I mean: it is not based on grounds. It is not reasonable (or unreasonable). It is there—like our life" (*OC*, §559). I think that this extraordinary remark is particularly helpful for the clarification of what I can finally call Wittgenstein's joint vision of language and life. One may also call it his *biological* vision, but only if one thinks about "bio-logy" as the coming together of life (*bios*) and language (*logon*). At first sight, there is something quite peculiar about the oracular statement that the language-game "is there [*da*]—like our life." If I would be pressed to answer the question, "What is there?" (a rather obscure question from a Wittgensteinian point of view), I guess that I would speak about certain facts in the world around me (for example, "The building is on fire," "There are people in the streets," etc.). But in what sense could something like language, or life, be said to be "there"? The answer, which might sound even more odd than the question itself, is that by *presenting* our language-games and our forms of life, we make them, in some sense, present in the world. It seems that what Wittgenstein wants us to realize is that what we do and what we say, how we act and how we live, is always, in a certain sense, "out there," like facts in the world. This "factical" nature of our language and our life, their "thereness," which appears at first sight to be arbitrary and groundless, beyond explanations, justifications, and reasons, is another way of understanding what has to be accepted, this given, which Wittgenstein calls "forms of life."

It is fascinating to see how the seed of this radical thought, which manifests itself only in the last stage of Wittgenstein's philosophical development, is already there from the very beginning. I mentioned earlier that the world in the *Tractatus* is presented as the totality of facts, and I suggested that toward the end of his life these facts are perceived not merely as objective facts in the world but as what he calls "facts of living." But it is important to add that any fact, a *Tatsache*, is not a mere entity, or *Sache*, because it also contains a deed, a *Tat* (as in English "fact" is derived from the Latin *"facere,"* to do). Every *Tatsache* is therefore a *Tat-Sache*, literally, a deed-entity, or an entity of the deed. A fact is inseparable from what we can *do*. In the beginning (of Wittgenstein's philosophy) there is not merely a word or a proposition, a *logos* or a law, but also what one does, how one lives. This is the reason why forms of life and facts of life, facts of living and facts in the world, cannot be told apart. In short, "The world and life are one" (*TLP*, §5.621).

6.4

A point that seems to escape many readers of *On Certainty*, the remarks Wittgenstein composed toward the end of his life, remarks that can properly be described as his philosophical Last Word, is their strong theological undertone. I believe that the observation that every problem in Wittgenstein's philosophy can be seen "from a religious point of view" (as Wittgenstein himself once suggested) makes sense more than anywhere else when it comes to these final considerations (Drury 1981: 94). Nevertheless, this approach should be qualified right away in order to avoid misunderstandings. First, it is important to realize that a philosophy seen from a religious point of view is not a religion seen from a philosophical point of view. You need to clarify Wittgenstein's philosophical project by attending to his religious sensibility and not the other way around. "Theology as grammar"—this is how he puts it in the *Investigations* (*PI*, §373). In this respect, theology is not the subject matter of his philosophical work, but, in some sense, the grammar of his work. Second, one must understand that Wittgenstein's religious sensibility is radically different from the set of beliefs that we are familiar with from institutional religion. For this reason, any attempt to look at Wittgenstein's philosophy from a religious point of view must search for *Wittgenstein's* religious point of view. You will therefore do best if you avert from traditional theological categories or references and focus only on the few unique remarks Wittgenstein makes about this sensitive and decisive subject in his own writings.[48]

Let me begin by asking candidly: What is religion? This simple question can also be answered without much ado. For Wittgenstein, religion needs to be conceived as a way, or a form, of life.[49] "It strikes me," he once wrote, "that a religious belief could only be something like a passionate commitment to a system of reference. Hence, although it's *belief*, it's really a way of living [*Art des Lebens*], or a way of assessing life" (*CV*, 64). Like philosophy, religion is neither a theory nor a doctrine, but it is an activity. From a Wittgensteinian point of view, it seems futile to advance theses in religion (like, "There is a God," or "The world was created in six days"), because then it would never be possible to debate these propositions, and everybody would have to agree on them. Instead, he claims that religion "is not a doctrine, not, I mean, a theory about what has happened and will happen to the human soul, but a description of something that actually takes place in human life" (*CV*, 28). As a consequence, anyone who wishes to understand the variety of religious experience should not look for laws, maxims, or dogmas. "I believe," Wittgenstein writes, "that sound doctrines are all useless," "that sound doctrine need not *take hold* of you," that "you can follow it as you would a doctor's prescription" (*CV*, 53). At the end of the day, there is really only one possible "doctrine" that religion can offer: "That you have to change your *life*. (Or the *direction* of your life)" (*ibid.*). Recall that Wittgenstein once told his pupil, "I don't try to make you *believe* something you *don't* believe, but to make you *do* something you won't do" (Rhees 1970: 43). Now you can see that this is not only the exclusive task of philosophy but also the task of religious teaching as well. Even though a form of life is what has to be accepted, we also have the ability to scrutinize, confront, critique, judge, or change a form of life. Maybe this is what Stanley Cavell calls, plain and simple, "philosophy." According to him, Wittgenstein's idea that "to imagine a language means to imagine a form of life" comes down to the following: "In philosophizing, I have to bring my own language and life into imagination" (Cavell 1979: 125). It is more difficult to think about religion in these radical terms, yet this is what I take Wittgenstein to stand for.

It can be said that the only religion that interests Wittgenstein is a religion within the bounds of life alone. It seems that only "life can educate one to a belief in God;" that only "life can force this concept on us" (*CV*, 86). Because this view of religion does not operate merely within the bounds of cold reason, but within the wider bounds of life, the problem is not necessarily that "one form of life culminates in an utterance of belief in a Last Judgment" (*LC*, 58). For Wittgenstein, the problem is that we fail to see that any attempt to justify a religious belief, like any attempt to justify anything whatsoever within a form of life, must reach the inevitable point where, indeed, explanations come to an end. If we take seriously the link between a religion and a form of life, then we no longer need to pretend that religion is reasonable, but neither do we need to assume that it is unreasonable. This is the main difficulty that Wittgenstein had with *The Golden Bough,* James Frazer's celebrated anthropological study of magic and religion. The way by which Frazer presents certain beliefs and practices as "primitive," as the mark of a low level of intellectual and scientific development, is seen by Wittgenstein to be nothing but the mark of "a narrow spiritual life on Frazer's part," since it was utterly impossible for the anthropologist "to conceive of a life different from that of the England of his time" (*PO*, 125). In other words, a religion within the bounds of life is a religion within the bounds of a *particular kind* of life, the kind of life in which the words, the deeds, and the beliefs find their home. Separated from a form of life, religious beliefs are not wrong; they are merely nonsensical.

Recall that Wittgenstein regards certainty not as hastiness and not as superficiality but as a form of life. Here is where the theological grammar reveals its worth. *Certainty is to form of life what faith is to religion:* "If I am to be REALLY saved," Wittgenstein can therefore write, "what I need is *certainty*—not wisdom, dreams or speculation—and this certainty is faith" (*CV*, 33). To think about certainty from a religious point of view is to think about it as faith—as a kind of a saving power in a world strewn with doubt. But in order to properly comprehend this idea, you must also attend to Wittgenstein's unique understanding of faith. Here, it is worthwhile to begin by following his distinction between faith and superstition: "Religious faith and superstition are quite different. One of them results from *fear* and is a sort of false science. The other is trusting" (*CV*, 72). Accordingly, we may say that Wittgenstein's understanding of certainty does not result from the *fear* that without this certainty our language and our life will sink into chaotic meaninglessness but because certainty is for him a sort of *trust*. The difference between fear and trust is not that fear is the assumption that something will go wrong while trust is the assumption that everything will be just fine. The difference can be described thus: fear is the assumption that if something will go wrong you will have no one to rely on; trust, on the other hand, is the assumption that you *do* have someone to rely on. Trust, in this respect, has nothing to do with the "trust" that one might have in the benevolence of nature, God, or the state, nor is it the "trust" in one's senses or one's reason. To call our reliance on such things "trust" is like confusing superstition with faith or like confusing a struggling certainty with a comfortable one. The trust Wittgenstein speaks about is the mutual trust between living beings. A form of life does not arise from fear but only from this comfortable shared trust. "I really want to say," he writes toward the end of *On Certainty*, "that a language-game is only possible if one trusts someone (I did not say 'can trust someone')" (*OC*, §509).[50]

6.5

Recall, however, that Wittgenstein regards certainty not only as a form of life but also as something that lies beyond being justified or unjustified, as something animalistic. This view can also be explained from a religious point of view if we consider another one of Wittgenstein's striking remarks on Frazer's *Golden Bough*, which will help us to see this animalistic nature at the basis of every certainty and every faith:

> There can have been no *reason* [*Grund*] that prompted certain races of mankind to venerate the oak tree, but only the fact that they and the oak were united in a community of life [*Lebensgemeinschaft*], and thus that they arose together not by choice, but rather like the flea and the dog. (If fleas developed a rite, it would be based on the dog.) (*PO*, 139)

I think that there is something quite intriguing about the idea of a "community of life"—this sort of a cohabitation, which is based on a factical situation in which different living beings, like humans and trees, or fleas and dogs, share the same environment. The participants in this community of life do not need to belong to the same species or the same race. No reason, no ground, no law, no contract, and no love are necessary for the possibility of such a community. Oak trees and men, fleas and dogs, do not agree on the language that they use, and it would certainly be a stretch to say that they have an agreement in form of life. But somehow they do share a life; they share a world. As prehistoric men and oak trees partook in the same "community," modern men who raise pets in their homes may be said to establish a certain community of life with their dogs, cats, and, of course, the fleas that their cats and dogs carry on their bodies from time to time. But you can also think about a city like New York, where so many different living beings dwell in the same small place, while the only thing that they have in common is that they have nothing in common (besides, that is, the city itself), and see here an excellent example for a community of life.

Wittgenstein, however, cannot be satisfied with this idyllic myth of a community of life, with its unmediated connection between different living beings, because he comes to realize that such a community does not really explain how religious rites can emerge. He therefore continues by describing how this original community of life is severed:

> One could say that it was not their union (the oak and man) that has given rise to these rites, but in a certain sense their separation. For the awakening of the intellect occurs with a separation from the original *soil*, the original basis [*Grundlage*] of life. (*ibid.*)

As objects become sacred by being separated from their everyday use, and concepts become metaphysical when alienated from ordinary language, things are venerated due to their detachment from the original basis, or ground, of life. You may very well consider as inconsequential this curious little myth about the initiation of religious rites as a result of the division of the community of life. I think, however, that it hints at a very interesting possibility. It may help you to understand Wittgenstein's last remarks on the subject of certainty in a new light. Reading many of these final remarks, you might be tempted to think that our forms of life, like our language-games, are, so to speak, forsaken. Time and again, you find those seemingly hopeless statements like: "The difficulty is to realize the groundlessness of our believing"; "At the foundation of well-founded belief lies belief that is not founded"; "If the true is what is grounded, then the ground is not *true*, nor yet false"; "But the end is not an ungrounded presupposition: it is an ungrounded way of acting" (*OC*, §§ 110, 166, 205, 253). Yet if you conclude that everything that we say, do, and believe is essentially arbitrary, then you simply need to go back and examine this "original ground of life" at the end of the Wittgensteinian myth. In this way, you can see that the groundlessness of what we do, what we say, and what we believe has something to do with the separation from the ground that lies before us, this is to say, the ground of life. Life is simply there, in plain view, and this is what we seem in some sense not to understand. But this life, which lies *before* us—and should therefore not be confused with a metaphysical ground that lies deep down or up high—cannot be considered as true, nor yet as false, as it is neither reasonable nor unreasonable, neither justified nor unjustified. After all, "it is life that justifies; it has no need of being justified" (Deleuze 1997: 81). In contrast to what the above consideration concerning Wittgenstein's "religious point of view" may tempt you to believe, certainty is not a *blind* acceptance of ungrounded words, deeds, and beliefs. In the same way that substantial trust and real faith are never blind, true certainty, comfortable certainty, can only be obtained when your words, deeds, and beliefs are deeply rooted in the soil of a shared life, profoundly embedded in a community of life.

6.6

And so, whatever I know, whatever is not mere rumbling and roaring that I have heard, can be said in three words: *attend to life*. But, of course, even these three words are rather pointless, since such an attention cannot come into being by expressing a simple proposition in language, as love never begins by uttering the words, "I love you," as happiness is not the result of saying, "Live happily" (*NB*, 78). Because for Wittgenstein, "the world of the happy man is a different one from that of the unhappy man," as the world of those who are in love is different from the world of those who fall out of love, as the world that is one with life is quite another than a world that is separated from life (*TLP*, §6.43). Our experience of life, love, and happiness shows us that the world must, somehow, become "an altogether different world. It must, so to speak, wax and wane as a whole" (*ibid.*). And so, since there is really not much that is left to be said, I must bring this book to its end. Let me, then, conclude with a quote that is not taken from Wittgenstein. It comes from the Bible. In first reading, it may sound hollow or simply foreign. But I think that if you will look at it closely, you will see that it is actually quite straightforward and close to Wittgenstein's spirit. Toward the conclusion of the Torah, in the end of their exodus, at the gate of their promised land, on the threshold of their coming community, Moses tells his people:

> For the commandment that I command you today is not hidden from you, and it is not far away. It is not in heaven, so do not say, "Who will go up to the sky and bring it to us that we may hear it, and do it?" And it is not beyond the sea, so do not say, "Who will cross to the other side of the water and get it for us that we may hear it, and do it?" Because this thing is very near to you: it is in your mouth and it is in your heart for you to do it. (Deuteronomy 30:11–4, my translation)

Then, at the very end of Moses' speech, he enounces: "I call today as your witnesses the heaven and the earth. Life and death I have set before you, the blessing and the cursing. And now choose life, so that you and your children may live" (*ibid.* 30:19).

Epilogue: Threshold

Since the publication of *Philosophical Investigations*, shortly after Wittgenstein's death, a few attempts were made to direct our attention toward the importance of the concept of form of life in his writings. In an early review of the book, Norman Malcolm observed that "one could hardly place too much stress" on the importance of "form of life" in Wittgenstein's thought (Malcolm 1954: 549). A few years later, Stanley Cavell helped us to notice

> our sharing routes of interest and feeling, modes of response, senses of humor and of significance and of fulfillment, of what is outrageous, of what is similar to what else, what a rebuke, what forgiveness, of when an utterance is an assertion, when an appeal, when an explanation—all the whirl of organism Wittgenstein calls "form of life." Human speech and activity, sanity and community, rest upon nothing more, but nothing less, than this. It is a vision as simple as it is (and because it is) terrifying. (Cavell 1962: 74)

To a great extent, this is the simple yet terrifying vision I was trying to promote in this book. Nevertheless, if you recognize the potential power of the concept of form of life, and you wish to have a better grasp of its meaning by examining the prodigious scholarly work dedicated to it, you will discover a curious phenomenon. Virtually every attempt to explain what exactly "Wittgenstein means" when he uses this notion takes the same path. First of all, there is a general agreement that, given the scanty mentions of "form of life" in the manuscripts, this term remains quite opaque and impenetrable. As Max Black explains,

> One might compare Wittgenstein's reference to a *"Lebensform"* [form of life] with the practice of old map-makers who labeled unexplored areas as "Terra Incognita." Or one might say that the

word "*Lebensform*" marks a *contour* of Wittgenstein's elaborated investigations. For, as an ancient writer [Pliny] said, a contour ought to suggest the presence of things partly hidden and not yet fully disclosed. (Black 1978: 330)

But while Black concludes his analysis with this gesture, most scholars continue after their initial admittance of the ambivalence of this concept to make their own speculations as to what the precise meaning of "form of life" in Wittgenstein's work is. At this point, we can again trace a recurring pattern. First, a group of scholars will argue that Wittgenstein's use of "form of life" supports a certain thesis, a certain worldview, or a certain "ism." Then, another group of scholars will promote an interpretation of the *same* concept of form of life in order to make the exact *opposite* argument. In this way, the literature on the subject covers many of the familiar two-sided philosophical debates, while the concept of form of life somehow manages to support *both* sides of the argument. In the secondary literature, "form of life" may be likened to a chameleon—it changes its colors according to its background, according to the philosophical view at hand.

Let me sketch for you very briefly some of these familiar debates. First and foremost, we need to confront the ancient question of the one and the many, because it is never clear whether Wittgenstein speaks about *forms* of life or about *the* form of life. The problem is that if there is a multiplicity of forms of life, then how are they going to be divided (Whittaker 1978)? And if we deal with a single, usually human, form of life, then what does it include or exclude (Garver 1994)? On this ground, we can trace a second debate between those who speak about biological, organic, or natural forms of life in opposition to those who speak about cultural, social, or communal forms of life. According to the first view, forms of life separate different types of animals, and they constitute a sort of a natural history (Cavell 1989; Garver 1994). According to the other view, forms of life are meant to distinguish between different kinds of human beings, and they account for our cultural differences (Winch 1990; Lurie 1992). Where the first view focuses on the unity and necessity of the human form of life as a given that persists over time, the opposite view emphasizes the diversity and contingency of different human forms and the ability to alter such conventions. From here, a third debate arises between those who use Wittgenstein's notion of form of life in their argument for various strands of relativism and those who use the very same concept in their arguments against the relativist view. Relativists usually support the idea that a form of life is a form of culture, and they tend to claim that it is inviolable, that it cannot be criticized, and is never superior or inferior to other forms of life (Hilmy 1987; Rorty 1989; Emmett 1990). Anti-relativists (who are also called absolutists, objectivists, or transcendentalists) tend to see a coherent human form of life that goes beyond our differences by means of a shared reason or rationality (Lear 1982; Hinman 1983; Rudder-Baker 1984).[51] Another offshoot of the above considerations is a fourth debate between those who understand "form of life" from a conservative point of view and those who look at it from a liberal point of view. Conservatives take the existing form of life to be a sort of a solid entity that is, or needs to be, protected from rapid changes (Nyíri 1982; Bloor 1983). Liberals, on the other hand, take a form of life to be a much more fluid entity that can and should be mended (Rorty 1989; Robinson 2006). Where some resist any attempt to exert political power over a form of life, others take the force to shape a form of life to be the essence of politics. Where some take a form of life to be a-political in its nature, others take it to be the political power par excellence.[52]

As you can see, "form of life" resists the simple game of dichotomies, since it cannot be pinpointed to only one side of our dualistic way of thinking. Instead, it gives the illusion that it is both here and there. Trying to define the specific meaning of "form of life" is like trying to determine what is the true color of a chameleon or like trying to decide whether the following is a drawing of a duck or of a rabbit (*PI*, 194):

The problem, however, is that the seeming ambivalence of "form of life" not only explains nothing but is itself in need of explanation. It appears that "form of life" has reached this "moment in the life of concepts when they lose their immediate intelligibility and can then, like all empty terms, be overburdened with contradictory meanings" (Agamben 1998: 80). I therefore want to ask the following: Should this seeming contradiction tempt us to discard the notion of form of life? If Wittgenstein's use of "form of life" cannot endorse unequivocally a certain thesis, does it necessarily mean that the concept itself is problematic? Maybe our dichotomies are the problematic ones? Maybe our inclination to think about philosophy as a set of opposing doctrines or theories is the root of the problem? Could the anomaly that we detect every time we try to use this concept within our usual philosophical debates generate a paradigm shift that will help us to go beyond those simplistic dualistic arguments?

Following Wittgenstein's unique approach to language, this book made an effort to find meaningful ways of coping with the concept of form of life without reducing it to a simple definition, without accepting its ambivalence as a given, and without deeming the concept as nonsensical. By showing how Wittgenstein brings language into the sphere of life, this was also an attempt to show how life can be brought into the sphere of language. The strategy, however, was not to fixate, capture, or pin down the subject matter, but to keep it moving, to keep it alive, by investigating the many ways by which Wittgenstein uses the term "life" throughout his writings. Despite the prevalent inclination, I tried not to accept as a given one side of the standard dualistic divide. It was therefore an endeavor to prove that "life" is not an empty term but, indeed, an extremely rich, meaningful, and powerful one. I was trying to explain that even though you cannot represent a form of life, and you cannot make a picture of it, there is still a way to present a form of life, to imagine a form of life.

This, however, is far from saying that the extensive scholarly work on the subject was futile. In fact, I think that it can teach us a very important lesson about the unique position of "form of life" in today's thought. This position, I need to note, will take us to the limits of Wittgenstein's own thought and is offered here as a preliminary speculation for a future investigation. Let me take you, then, once again, on a short detour.

Toward the end of the *Tractatus*, Wittgenstein raises an old Kantian problem. How come a left hand and a right hand cannot coincide with each other? Why can't we wear the left-hand glove on our right hand and vice versa? In order to better understand this seemingly unproblematic problem, as well as its curious solution, we can simplify the matter from three-dimensional hands to lines in a single dimension. Look at these two arrows, *a* and *b*, which cannot be made to coincide with one another because of their opposite directions, unless they are taken out of their single dimension and turned in a two-dimensional space:

The same problem arises when we begin with two-dimensional figures, like the following scripts that mirror each other. But they can also be made to coincide if we add the third dimension of depth and flip them as if we were closing an open book:

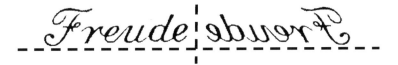

This insight allows Wittgenstein to explain that in fact the right hand and the left hand, which exist in a three-dimensional space, are completely congruent as well: "A right-hand glove could be put on the left hand, if it could be turned round in four-dimensional space" (*TLP*, §6.36111).

But what is the "fourth dimension" of which Wittgenstein speaks? In opposition to a widespread belief, the fourth dimension is not time. The passage of time cannot transform a left glove to a right glove. Think, however, once again about the left-hand glove that can be turned round in a four-dimensional space. What Wittgenstein fails to mention is that this seemingly fantastic maneuver is in fact quite ordinary. How can you turn a left-hand glove into a right-hand glove? It was rather surprising to realize, as I was playing with one of my gloves on a cold winter day, the simplicity of the solution: *just turn the glove inside out.* Imagine that you place a living being on the zero point of a system of coordinates. Intuitively, if the first, horizontal, dimension (x) allows this living being to move right and left, the second, vertical, dimension (y) up and down, and the third, sagittal, dimension (z) forward and back, then it follows that the fourth dimension must enable this living being to move in and out. From this perspective, the zero point of the fourth dimension (call it the ℵ dimension, if you like) is a threshold from which one can move inside or outside, inwards or outwards.[53]

I believe that a basic gesture in Wittgenstein's philosophy is the gesture of turning the glove inside out. In both his early and later writings, he shows you that the inside is not separated from the outside by an impassable limit but by a threshold on a continuum. The idea that the inside and outside constitute two distinct zones is shown to make as much sense as the idea that right and left are two different realms. In this way, Wittgenstein enables you to see how two things that give the impression that they cannot be made to coincide may actually be completely congruent. But instead of offering the synthesis of a thesis and its antithesis, he shows how a thesis (the left glove) can easily be transformed into its antithesis (the right glove). All that needs to be done is to make from what is inside an outside and what is outside an inside.

A good example for this curious maneuver can be traced back to Wittgenstein's notebooks from World War I, where he describes "the way I have traveled," this is to say, the itinerary of his thought, by claiming that "idealism leads to realism if it is strictly thought out" (*NB*, 85). This is how he puts it in the *Tractatus*:

> Here it can be seen that solipsism, when its implications are followed out strictly, coincides with pure realism. The self of solipsism shrinks to a point without extension, and there remains the reality co-ordinated with it. (*TLP*, §5.64)

In other words, the inner world of the idealists and the external world of the realists are congruent as long as they pass through solipsism, which marks a threshold, or a zero point without extension, which Wittgenstein calls the "philosophical self" (*TLP*, §5.641). But instead of taking this self to be a mirror of the facts that lies outside or a reflection of the experience that hides inside, instead of placing this self in the external world as a body or in the internal world as a soul, we may represent the way Wittgenstein's thought has traveled as follows:

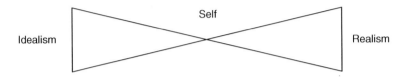

This attitude becomes even more apparent in Wittgenstein's later writings, where you come to acknowledge the problem in committing language to the task of being a mirror of the objective world or a reflection of your subjective thought. Instead, Wittgenstein shows you that what is external and what is internal, what is outside and what is inside, are completely congruent as long as they pass through the surface of language. Language is the point where the distinction of inside and outside simply breaks down. From this perspective, it is senseless to speak about "the threshold of language," because language is itself nothing but a sort of a threshold. "The limits of language," beyond which one cannot speak, shrink to a point without extension, and there remain the internal and external realities coordinate with it:

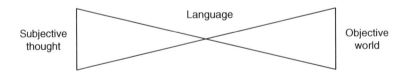

I would like to make now the transition from imagining a language to imagining a form of life one last time, in order to explain the importance of my strange excursus. As you have seen, the secondary literature on "form of life" constantly utilizes this term in a series of attempts to explain completely opposite and seemingly incongruent views, like the one and the many, nature and culture, absolutism and relativism, conservatism and liberalism. In all those debates you can clearly see how "form of life" never simply occupies one side of the dualism but its point of convergence. It never gives in to one theory or doctrine. "Form of life" is neither the left-hand glove nor the right-hand glove. It is, so to speak, the fourth dimension where the glove is turned inside out. It enables things that seem incongruent to coincide. It renders our dualistic divisions inoperative. It shows us that all those theories and doctrines are vacuous. It solves problems by dissolving them. For example, throughout this book, I was trying to show that it is in form of life, and in form of life alone, that "the world" and "life" could be said to be "one." But the list of traditional dichotomies that can be reevaluated in this way can easily be extended. I would only like to indicate in the direction of two possibilities that informed this research all along: First, that the concept of form of life can help you to reconsider the separation between Wittgenstein's early and later philosophies. Second, that the concept of form of life is a crucial point of contact between Anglo-American and Continental philosophies.

While I hope that the attempt to go beyond the separation into the "early" and the "later" Wittgenstein manifested itself throughout this book, the second possibility must somehow be clarified in these closing, speculative, remarks. In order to point toward this bridge between Anglo-American and Continental thought, I will need to turn now to the publication of a short essay by the contemporary Italian philosopher, Giorgio Agamben, entitled "Form-of-life." Without even mentioning Wittgenstein's name, this essay marks the beginning of a remarkable investigation that opens the door to a radically new way of thinking about the Wittgensteinian notion of form of life, which, according to Agamben, "must become the guiding concept and the unitary center of the coming politics" (Agamben 2000: 12). In another essay from the same period, he will go as far as saying that "the concept of life must constitute the subject of the coming philosophy" (Agamben 1999: 238).[54]

These bold statements are based on Agamben's realization that what we mean today by the single term "life" can be traced back to two distinct notions in Ancient Greek: *zoé*, which signifies the fact of life, and *bios*, which is the form of life. The Greeks reserved matters pertaining to the mere fact of living, this is to say, to our natural or biological existence, for the realm of the *oikos*, or the home. On the other hand, the form or the manner of living of individuals and groups was always considered to be a political question, exclusive to the sphere of the *polis*, or the city. But this idyllic depiction of the Greeks' separation of life into *bios* and *zoé* in the two distinct zones of the *polis* and the *oikos* is not the end of Agamben's story. It is, rather, the beginning of a disturbing tale about our current political situation. By continuing the works of Hannah Arendt and Michel Foucault, Agamben shows that today we are witnessing the irrevocable *dissolution* of this ancient separation of life. In a seminar conducted at Princeton in 2001, Agamben illustrated this point by drawing on the board the following diagram:

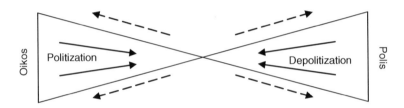

This is what Agamben calls the "biopolitical machine," which works in two directions: first, it takes the natural fact of living out of its place in the home and exposes it in the public sphere; second, it retracts the form of life from politics, making from it a mere private affair. In short, it politicizes the *oikos* and de-politicizes the *polis*. The consequence of this dynamic process, the great danger behind this biopolitical machine, is something that Agamben calls "naked life"— *a life that is stripped from its form.* Unlike the Greek *zoé*, this bare life constitutes the center of modern politics, which no longer cares for our form of life but simply for this naked fact of living. Since our understanding of life is always based on this division into private and public, biological body and body politic, *zoé* and *bios*, there is an imminent threat that our various forms of life will be reduced to the single naked fact of being alive, thus revealing the secret foundation of biopolitics. Agamben sees the paradigmatic embodiment of this process in the *muselmann*, an inhabitant of the Nazis' death camps who was separated from the human form of life to the point at which he even lost the capacity to speak, to resist pain, and to ask for food. The meaning of all those theoretical formulations is therefore a place called Auschwitz (Agamben 1998).

My book was written as a reaction to the great danger inherent in this reduction of a form of life to a mere fact, to this exposure to violence of a *life without language*. But it was motivated by the hope that where there is danger, there also grows that which saves. Look again at Agamben's diagram. At its center, it is no longer possible to clearly separate life between the *oikos* and the *polis*, between the home and the city, between an inside and an outside. As the left glove can become a right glove and the right glove can become a left glove by being turned inside out, this is also the point where the simple distinction of *zoé* and *bios* loses its force. Exactly at this zone of indistinction we can place the Agambenian notion of "form-of-life." He hyphenates this concept in order to stress that form-of-life, unlike the Greek *bios*, is a new image of "a life that can never be separated from its form, a life in which it is never possible to isolate something such as naked life" (Agamben 2000: 3–4). Then he explains, in a passage that I have utilized time and again throughout this book:

> A life that cannot be separated from its form is a life for which what is at stake in its way of living is living itself. What does this formulation mean? It defines a life—human life—in which the single ways, acts, and processes of living are never simply *facts* but always and above all *possibilities* of life, always and above all power. (*ibid.*)

For Agamben, "form-of-life" is the point in which nature and culture, the natural biological life and the qualified political life, find themselves suspended in a zone of indistinction. It is the awareness to this zone that becomes the starting point for what he takes to be the coming political activity and a new philosophical thought. Standing on the threshold between the living being and the speaking being, form-of-life is the locus in which it is no longer possible to think of bodies without words, or words without bodies. In this medium, language and life constitute a force field in which form-of-life finds its proper dwelling place:

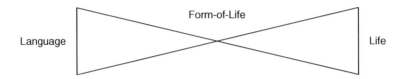

The presence of Agamben's work in virtually every single page of this book should not be missed. But to make this implicit force explicit—to transform the wind in the sails into the sails themselves—goes beyond the scope of this investigation. Of course, if one wishes to say something, one must say it clearly. This, then, will be the next step in my attempt to imagine a form of life.

Notes

Introduction

[1] Plato, *Phaedo*: 64a. It seems rather obvious that Plato, and not Socrates, is responsible for this claim. As Hannah Arendt observes,

> In the *Apology* as in other cases, Socrates is saying very nearly the opposite of what Plato made him say in the "improved apology" of the *Phaedo*. In the *Apology*, Socrates tells his fellow-citizens why he should live and also why, though life is "very dear" to him, he is not afraid of death; in the *Phaedo*, he explains to his friends how burdensome life is and why he is glad to die. (Arendt 1978: 172)

And now notice how Derrida, two months before his death, neither affirms nor rejects Plato's claim, as he literally wrestles with it:

> So, to finally answer your question, no, I never learned-to-live. In fact not at all! Learning to live should mean learning to die, learning to take into account, so as to accept, absolute mortality (that is, without salvation, resurrection, or redemption – neither for oneself nor for the other). That's been the old philosophical injunction since Plato: to philosophize is to learn to die. I believe in this truth without being able to resign myself to it. And less and less so. I have never learned to accept it, to accept death, that is. (Derrida 2007: 24)

[2] I will return to the link between the concept of life and the concept of God at the end of the third and the sixth chapters.

[3] Similarly to Wittgenstein, Spinoza writes in the *Ethics*: "A free man thinks of death least of all things, and his wisdom is a meditation of life, not of death" (Spinoza 1991: 193).

[4] About a decade after the *Tractatus*, Martin Heidegger claims in *Being and Time* that the concept of life is never understood in an adequate manner. In the tenth section of the book, "How the analytic of Da-sein is to be distinguished from anthropology, psychology, and biology," he goes against the tendency to reduce "life" to a psychological or a physiological fact (Heidegger 1996: 42–7). This inadequacy is the force behind his decision to distinguish the human life by calling it "Da-sein," or being-there, and characterizing it as a being that is

always already "thrown" into the world. Da-sein could only be understood by an appeal to this world; it is always a "being-in-the-world." This is also the reason why, for Heidegger, the experience of death, or, as he calls it, "no-longer-being-in-the-world" (or, if you like, "no-longer-being-in-life") is what helps Da-sein to face its authentic being. We may say that for Heidegger "being-in-life" is meaningful only insofar as it is understood as a "being-in-the-world," exactly because, as Wittgenstein claims, the world and life are one.

[5] It is important to note that Aristotle offers much more than an isolated definition:

> Now, that man is more of a political animal than bees or any other gregarious animal is evident. Nature, as we often say, makes nothing in vain, and man is the only animal who has the gift of speech. And whereas mere voice is but an indication of pleasure and pain, and is therefore found in other animals (for their nature attains to the perception of pleasure and pain and the intimation of them to one another, and no further), the power of speech is intended to set forth the expedient and inexpedient, and therefore likewise the just and the unjust. And it is a characteristic of man that he alone has any sense of good and evil, of just and unjust, and the like, and the association of living beings who have this sense make a family and a state. (*The Politics*: 1253a 7–18)

Chapter 1

[6] I am following here Cora Diamond's understanding of formal concepts, which is one of the pillars for her reading of Wittgenstein's *Tractatus* (Diamond 1991: 194–8).

[7] Eli Friedlander's link between form and possibility constitutes the first decisive move in his own reading of the *Tractatus* (Friedlander 2001: 34–46).

[8] Michael Thompson shows the futility of the empiricist's attempt to observe life as a fact or as a thing. But instead of leaving this concept of life as a lacuna in our thought, he indicates that life could still be understood as a formal concept, or as a logical space, as I will try to show in what follows (Thompson 1995 and 2004).

[9] In "The unity of Wittgenstein's philosophy," Peter Winch claims that the later Wittgenstein will not abandon his earlier ideas about logic but will reassess them in view of his new understanding of language-games and forms of life (Winch 1969). Wittgenstein will become aware of the metaphysical insistence inherent in a single logical space in which, or a single logical form by which, whatever we say and think makes sense. As we will see in Chapter 2, he came to realize that the persistence of the idea of a general propositional form is indeed a metaphysical commitment to which he was blind as he was writing the *Tractatus*. Yet I still believe that his original understanding of form remains the seed for many later developments that will be presented as we go along.

[10] This attitude is inspired by what Cora Diamond takes to be Wittgenstein's "realistic spirit." To have a realistic spirit, according to Diamond, is not to be

a realist, in the epistemological sense of the word. In opposition to a meta-physical spirit, which always tries to ground our lives, a realistic spirit constantly searches for how we actually live. This realistic spirit is, therefore, an *ethical* comportment that always attends to what is actually the case in the world around us (Diamond 1991: 39–72).

[11] On this encounter between Russell and Wittgenstein, see James Conant's "On going the bloody hard way in philosophy" (Conant 2002).

Chapter 2

[12] What is today called "the correspondence theory of truth," dates back to the medieval understanding of *ens creatum*, created things (e.g. a sentence, a life) as true only insofar as they correspond to the *intellectus divinus*, that is, to God's mind (Heidegger 1993: 118).

[13] "What is your aim in philosophy? – To show the fly the way out of the fly-bottle" (*PI*, §309).

[14] "We have a false idea of how our thready, knotty lives can stand in relation to the rigor of logic, the bindingness of ethics, the necessity of mathematics. We are dazzled, Wittgenstein says, by ideals, and fail to understand their role in our language" (Diamond 1991: 36).

[15] This was in fact the method that the art historian Aby Warburg used in his attempt to compile a mammoth picture-atlas that was meant to contain variations of images throughout the ages on particular themes (Warburg 2000).

[16] James Conant presented this photo in a lecture at the University of Bergen in 2005. I thank him for a copy of this image, which is catalogued as item #598 at the Wittgenstein Archive in Cambridge.

[17] A proper interpretation of the theory of ideas cannot be offered here, but let me only suggest the following: as medicine is not the science of this or that health, but of health without qualification, this is to say, health itself, we could say that what Plato took to be at stake in the form of our lives is not this or that way of living but life without qualifications, this is to say, living itself.

[18] From this perspective, the law is also connected to what Wittgenstein calls at the end of the *Tractatus* "the mystical" – what cannot be put into words, although it makes itself manifest (*TLP*, §6.522). Whether Scholem, the scholar of Jewish mysticism, and Wittgenstein speak about the same mystical experience remains an open question. But one may still find interest in the curious fact that Scholem attended Frege's lectures at the same time that Wittgenstein was working on the *Tractatus* (Scholem 2001: 61).

Chapter 3

[19] The stream of life: *PR*, 81; *Z*, §173; *RPPII*, §§504, 687; *LWPPI*, §913; *LWPPII*, 30. Patterns in the weave of life: *Z*, §568–9; *PI*, 174, 229; *RPPII*, §§672–3; *LWPPI*, §§206, 211, 365, 406, 862; *LWPPII*, 26–7, 40, 42. Being embedded in life: *RPPII* §§16, 150. The bustle of life: *RPPII*, §625–6. The flux of life: *LWPPI*, §246.

Concepts find their home within our life: *RPPII*, §186. Rupert Read and James Guetti are skeptical about the importance of life for Wittgenstein's understanding of meaning. They attribute the idea of the "stream of life" to Norman Malcolm and overlook the textual evidences from Wittgenstein's manuscripts mentioned above. They are correct, however, in claiming that the appeal to this stream of life leaves the notion of meaning rather vague. This chapter is an attempt to be as concrete as the subject matter permits about the link of meaning to life (Read and Guetti 1999).

[20] Caleb Thompson draws our attention to the connection between Tolstoy's book and Wittgenstein's *Tractatus* (Thompson 1997). Another helpful account of Wittgenstein's early philosophy of life and its link to Tolstoy can be found in Yuval Lurie's *Tracking the Meaning of Life: A Philosophical Journey* (Lurie 2006). I try here to continue this line of investigation by placing Tolstoy's confession in the seemingly unrelated context of Wittgenstein's later writings.

[21] "Augustine, we might say, does describe a system of communication; only not everything that we call language is this system" (*PI*, §3).

[22] "The general notion of the meaning of a word surrounds the working of language with a haze which makes clear vision impossible" (*PI*, §5).

[23] Stanley Cavell dwells on this complicated link between Augustine's *Confessions* and Wittgenstein's *Investigations* (Cavell 1995). But it is also possible to simplify this relationship by following Caleb Thompson's understanding of Wittgenstein's *Investigations* as nothing but a sort of a philosophical confession in its own right (Thompson 2000).

[24] The main difference between the thought of Wittgenstein and that of Ferdinand de Saussure is the latter's insistence on the duality of *langue* and *parole*, the abstract structure of language and its actual manifestation. In Wittgenstein, this distinction makes little or no sense. Here you can also see why the talk about form of life has little to do with what people usually refer to in various disciplines as "formalism."

[25] Wittgenstein could not have known at the time he wrote this sentence that, a few years later, he will help his extremely affluent family to dispense much of its fortune in order to be saved from the Nazis' claws.

[26] Karl Marx's depiction of the shift from use value to exchange value, and the creation of what he calls "the fetishism of commodity," may be connected to Wittgenstein's comment about the cow, the money, and its use. From this perspective, Wittgenstein's project can be seen as an attempt to fight against the "fetishistic" character of our language, or the "bewitchment" by our words, which leads to the consideration of meaning as a mysterious phenomenon and to the separation of words from their simple use value (*Z*, §690). Could this be "the most consequential" influence of Piero Sraffa, the Marxist economist, on Wittgenstein's thought (*PI*, Preface)? For more on this topic, see "Wittgenstein and Marx on philosophical language" (Read 2000), as well as "Gramsci, Sraffa, Wittgenstein: Philosophical linkages" (Davis 2002).

[27] On the link between touch and life, see Aristotle, *De anima*: 413b3–7; cf. Heidegger 1996: 51–2.

[28] I tell you [my soul] that you are already superior. For you animate the mass of your body and provide it with life, since no body is capable of doing that for

another body. But your God is for you the life of your life [*vitae vita*]." (Augustine, *Confessions*: Book 10, §6)

[29] Compare with the following quotes from Augustine's *Confessions*: "What Lord, do I wish to say except that I do not know whence I came to be in this mortal life or, as I may call it, this living death?" (Book 1, §6). "That was my kind of life. Surely, my God, it was no real life at all?" (Book 3, §2). "What could all this matter to me, true life, my God?" (Book 1, §17). "When I seek for you, my God, my quest is for the happy life. I will seek you that 'my soul may live'" (Book 10, §20). "May I not be my own life. On my own resources I lived evilly. To myself I was death. In you I am recovering life" (Book 12, §10).

Chapter 4

[30] In "Wittgenstein, Augustine, and the fantasy of ascent," Caleb Thompson shows how Wittgenstein, like Augustine, learns to stand the temptation to climb a ladder to the beyond (Thompson 2002). Nevertheless, he takes the two different quotations where Wittgenstein's discusses the metaphor of the ladder to show the shift in his attitude, while I try to stress their continuity.

[31] Maybe the same point can also be put as follows: "In every life there remains something unlived just as in every word there remains something unexpressed" (Agamben 1995: 93).

[32] In his last essay, Gilles Deleuze writes: "We will say of pure immanence that it is A LIFE, and nothing else. It is not immanence to life, but the immanence that is in nothing is itself a life. A life is the immanence of immanence, abso-lute immanence: it is complete power, complete bliss" (Deleuze 2001: 27).

[33] In "What 'ethics' in the *Tractatus* is *not*," James Conant gives a preliminary account of the way by which the resolute reading of the *Tractatus* may lead to what I call here a resolute view of life (Conant 2005).

[34] "The call upon history will seem uncongenial with Wittgenstein. He seems so ahistorical.—He is ahistorical the way Nietzsche is atheistical. (Call these desires for awakening)" (Cavell 1979: 370).

[35] S. K. Wertz suggests that when Wittgenstein uses the concept "form of life" he may be relying on Schopenhauer's original use of this term in *The World as Will and Idea*. Interestingly enough, Schopenhauer states in his book in more than one occasion that "the form of all life is the *present*," that "the form of life is an endless present," and that "the form of life, or the manifestation of the will with consciousness, is primarily and immediately merely the present" (quoted in Wertz 1981: 2).

[36] Roy Brand explains the matter in slightly different terms:

> Language harbors silence in the same way that life harbors death. Death is not a domain outside life but its own inner limit and there is nothing beyond . . . The end here is not a certain limit that cannot be passed through; it is not a wall and to view it as such is already to imagine ourselves capable of seeing beyond. What we reach here is not a limit but a threshold. (Brand 2004: 337)

[37] Cora Diamond rejects the "wholesale" versus "retail" approach to the difference between the early and the later Wittgenstein. She takes the novelty of Wittgenstein's later thought to lie in its ability to deal with a variety of questions while keeping in mind the background of the "big questions" from the early philosophy. In the same manner, I am not trying to ask or answer here *the* question of life, but only *questions* of life, without losing sight of the overarching subject matter. To use Diamond's phrase, I could say that a philosophy of life must be a "criss-cross philosophy" (Diamond 2004).

[38] In "Wittgenstein in relation to his times," G. H. von Wright explores this curious strand of remarks in Wittgenstein's manuscripts. He claims that Wittgenstein's philosophical "struggle with language" must be understood as grounded within a deeper struggle with ways of life (Wright 1982). Like von Wright, I do not assume a substantial distinction between a way of life, a mode of life, and a form of life.

Chapter 5

[39] For a discussion that continues along the line of Rhees' insight, see Cora Diamond's "Rules: Looking in the right place," where she claims that the confusion about Wittgenstein's idea of following a rule is "fed by the abstraction of 'agreement' from the life into which it is woven" (Diamond 1998: 33). She explains:

> We are brought into a life in which we rest on, depend on, people's following rules of many sorts, and in which people depend on us: rules, and agreement in following them, and reliance on agreement in following them, and criticizing or rounding on people who do not do it right – all this is woven in the texture of life; and it is in the context of its having a place in such a form of human life that a 'mistake' is recognizably that. (*ibid.*: 27–8)

[40] It may be worthwhile, though it may also be misleading, to consider the following ad hoc definitions: *Infancy* is a life that is not yet immersed in rules. *Law* is a rule that is no longer absorbed in lives. The space that opens up between infancy and law, where a rule and a life constantly interact with each other, is the space that Wittgenstein's later philosophy helps us to understand.

[41] "Precisely a philosophy of concrete life," a German jurist commented in 1934, "must not withdraw from the exception and the extreme case, but must be interested in it to the highest degree . . . In the exception the power of real life breaks through the crust of a mechanism that has become torpid by repetition" (Schmitt 2005: 15).

[42] Diamond criticizes Kripke precisely on this point. While Kripke thinks that if an isolated man would use the same mathematical rule as we do we could take him into our community, Diamond insists that a rule, and the criterion for its correctness or incorrectness, must be weaved into a shared life. While Kripke

sees a detached mathematical idea, Diamond sees this idea meshing with a life (Diamond 1998: 28–9).

[43] I am following here, as throughout this chapter, the basic gesture of Stephen Mulhall's analysis in *Wittgenstein's Private Language* (Mulhall 2007). Cora Diamond claims that the "private language argument" misleads us to think that speaking to oneself, playing a game with oneself, or writing in the diary for oneself, is really private, where in fact it is a continuation of the ways by which we are used to speaking and living. "Our life with others," she writes, "extends itself in various ways" (Diamond 1998: 30–1).

[44] "Happiness is a form of activity, and an activity clearly is something that comes into being, not a thing that we possess all the time, like a piece of property" (Aristotle, *The Nicomachean Ethics*: 1169b29).

[45] Eli Friedlander's analysis of the *Tractatus* distinguishes between *vorstellung* and *darstellung* by translating them as, respectively, presentation and representation (Friedlander 2001: 50–5). It is very problematic, however, to translate *vorstellung* as "presentation" every time it appears in the *Investigations*.

[46] Quoted in "Tolstoy and Wittgenstein as imitators of Christ" (Magnanini 1978). This is Tolstoy's reading of Mathew 5:15, but it is also a perfect gloss on John 1:4: "And life was the light of all people."

Chapter 6

[47] At this moment, even what Cavell calls "criteria" are not enough to justify our actions, because life, or a form of life, must be "the background against which our criteria do their work; even, make sense" (Cavell 1979: 83). For more on this subject, see his remarks on Kripke's reading of the *Investigations* (Kripke 1982; Cavell 1990). In this paragraph, the two characters, C and K, are meant to stand for Cavell and Kripke's positions.

[48] Norman Malcolm's posthumous monograph, *Wittgenstein: A Religious Point of View*, is an exemplary attempt to pursue this line of investigation (Malcolm 1994). Yet it seems that his argument is weakened by the double temptation to look at Wittgenstein's religion from a philosophical point of view as well as by his attempt to apply his reading to a variety of canonical texts and beliefs that exceed Wittgenstein's own religious experience.

[49] In his *Memoir*, Malcolm makes the following proposition: "I believe that [Wittgenstein] looked on religion as a 'form of life' (to use an expression from the *Investigations*) in which he did not participate, but with which he was sympathetic and which greatly interested him" (Malcolm 1970: 72). This claim is somewhat refined by Patrick Sherry, who explains that religion is not necessarily a *single* form of life, but a *cluster* of forms of life (praying, hoping, feeling certainty, believing, forgiving, feeling sin, worshipping, etc.). So religion is not a form of life, but it includes certain forms of life that may be considered "religious" but not necessarily (Sherry 1972).

[50] "I think," Malcolm writes, that Wittgenstein "means by this trust or acceptance what he calls belief 'in the sense of religious belief'" (Malcolm 1977: 204).

Epilogue

[51] Naomi Scheman shows in "Forms of life: Mapping the rough ground" the shortcomings of those who support and those who reject relativism (Scheman 1996).

[52] Alice Crary explains in "Wittgenstein's philosophy in relation to political thought" the problematic nature of the liberal–conservative debate when it confronts Wittgenstein's own thought (Crary 2000).

[53] Aristotle does not conceive directions as abstract but always as the directions of living beings: "above and below, right and left, front and back [but also inside and outside], are not to be looked for in all bodies alike, but only in those which, because living, contain within themselves a principle of motion; for in no part of inanimate object can we trace the principle of its motion" (*On the Heaven*: 284b31).

[54] Even though Agamben indicates that a deep understanding of language could facilitate a new comprehension of life, he rarely relies on Wittgenstein's work. He inherits from the tradition of Hegel, Heidegger, and Derrida, where instead of the link between *language* and *life* that I delineate in this study, Agamben traces a bond between the notions of *language* and *death*, as the title of one of his early books indicates (Agamben 1991).

Bibliography

Primary Sources

Wittgenstein, Ludwig. *Philosophical Investigations*. Second edition. Trans. G. E. M. Anscombe. Oxford: Blackwell, 1958. [*PI*]

—. *The Blue and Brown Books*. New York: Harper and Row, 1960. [*BB*]

—. *Tractatus Logico-Philosophicus*. Trans. David F. Pears and Brian F. McGuinness. London: Routledge and Kegan Paul Ltd, 1961. [*TLP*]

—. *Lectures and Conversations on Aesthetics, Psychology and Religious Belief*. Ed. Cyril Barrett. Oxford: Blackwell, 1966. [*LC*]

—. *Zettel*. Eds G. E. M. Anscombe and G. H. von Wright, trans. G. E. M. Anscombe. Oxford: Blackwell, 1967. [*Z*]

—. *Philosophical Grammar*. Ed. Rush Rhees, trans. Anthony Kenny. Berkley: University of California Press, 1974. [*PG*]

—. *Remarks on Colour*. Ed. G. E. M. Anscombe. Oxford: Blackwell, 1977. [*RC*]

—. *Remarks on the Foundations of Mathematics*. Eds G. H. von Wright, Rush Rhees, and G. E. M. Anscombe, trans. G. E. M. Anscombe. Oxford: Blackwell, 1978. [*RFM*]

—. *Notebooks 1914–1916*. Second edition. Eds G. H. von Wright and G. E. M. Anscombe, trans. G. E. M. Anscombe. Chicago: The University of Chicago Press, 1979. [*NB*]

—. *On Certainty*. Eds G. E. M. Anscombe and G. H. von Wright, trans. Denis Paul and G. E. M. Anscombe. Oxford: Blackwell, 1979. [*OC*]

—. *Wittgenstein and the Vienna Circle: Conversations Recorded by Friedrich Waismann*. Ed. Brian McGiunness, trans. J. Schulte and B. McGuinness. New York: Harper and Row Publishers, 1979. [*WVC*]

—. *Wittgenstein's Lectures, Cambridge 1932–35, from the Notes of Alice Ambrose and Margaret McDonald*. Ed. Alice Ambrose. Chicago: Chicago University Press, 1979. [*WLC*]

—. *Wittgenstein: Sources and Perspectives*. Ed. Allen Janik, trans. B. Gillette. Sussex: Harvester Press, 1979. [*WSP*]

—. *Culture and Value*. Eds G. H. von Wright and Heikki Nyman, trans. Peter Winch. Chicago: The University of Chicago Press, 1980. [*CV*]

—. *Philosophical Remarks*. Ed. Rush Rhees, trans. Raymond Hargreaves and Roger White. Chicago: The University of Chicago Press, 1980. [*PR*]

—. *Remarks on the Philosophy of Psychology, Vol. I*. Eds G. E. M. Anscombe and G. H. von Wright, trans. G. E. M. Anscombe. Oxford: Blackwell, 1980. [*RPPI*]

—. *Remarks on the Philosophy of Psychology, Vol. II.* Eds G. H. von Wright and Heikki Nyman, trans. C. G. Luckhardt and M. A. E. Aue. Oxford: Blackwell, 1980. [*RPPII*]

—. *Last Writings on the Philosophy of Psychology, Vol. I.* Eds G. H. von Wright and Heikki Nyman, trans. C. G. Luckhardt and M. A. E. Aue. Chicago: Chicago University Press, 1982. [*LWPPI*]

—. *Last Writings on the Philosophy of Psychology, Vol. II.* Eds G. H. von Wright and Heikki Nyman, trans. C. G. Luckhardt and M. A. E. Aue. Chicago: Chicago University Press, 1982. [*LWPPII*]

—. *Philosophical Occasions: 1912–1951.* Eds James Klagge and Alfred Nordmann. Indianapolis: Hackett Publishing, 1993. [*PO*]

Secondary Sources

Agamben, Giorgio. *Language and Death: The Place of Negativity.* Trans. Karen E. Pinkus and Michael Hardt. Minneapolis: University of Minnesota Press, 1991.

—. *Infancy and History: The Destruction of Experience.* Trans. Liz Heron. London: Verso, 1993.

—. *The Idea of Prose.* Trans. M. Sullivan and S. Whitsitt. Albany, NY: State University of New York Press, 1995.

—. *Homo Sacer: Sovereign Power and Bare Life.* Trans. Daniel Heller-Roazen. Stanford: Stanford University Press, 1998.

—. "Absolute immanence." In *Potentialities: Collected Essays in Philosophy*, trans. Daniel Heller-Roazen. Stanford: Stanford University Press, 1999, pp. 220–39.

—. "Form-of-life." In *Means Without End: Notes on Politics*, trans. Vincenzo Binetti and Cesare Casarino. Minneapolis: University of Minnesota Press, 2000, pp. 3–12.

—. *Profanations.* Trans. Jeff Fort. New York: Zone Books, 2007.

Arbus, Diane. *Revelations.* New York: Random House, 2003.

Arendt, Hannah. *The Life of the Mind, Vol. I: Thinking.* New York: Harcourt, 1978.

—. "What remains? The language remains." In *The Portable Hannah Arendt*, ed. Peter Baehr. New York: Penguin, 2000, pp. 3–22.

Aristotle. *The Nicomachean Ethics.* Trans. H. Rackham. Cambridge, MA: Harvard University Press, 1926.

—. *On the Heaven.* Trans. W. K. C. Guthrie. Cambridge, MA: Harvard University Press, 1939.

—. *De anima.* Trans. Hugh Lawson-Tancred. New York: Penguin, 1987.

—. *The Politics.* Ed. Stephen Everson. New York: Cambridge University Press, 1988.

Augustine. *Confessions.* Trans. Henry Chadwick. Oxford: Oxford University Press, 1998.

Benjamin, Walter. "Theses on the philosophy of history." In *Illuminations*, ed. Hannah Arendt. New York: Harcourt, 1968, pp. 253–64.

Bergson, Henri. *Creative Evolution.* Trans. Arthur Mitchell. New York: Modern Library, 1944.

Black, Max. "*Lebensborm* and *Sprachspiel* in Wittgenstein's later work." In *Wittgenstein and His Impact on Contemporary Thought, Vol. 2,* eds. E. Leinfellner, W. Leifellner, H. Berghel, and A. Hübner. Vienna: Holder-Pichler-Tempsky, 1978, pp. 325–31.

Bloor, David. *A Social Theory of Knowledge.* New York: Columbia University Press, 1983.

Brand, Roy. "Making sense speaking nonsense." *Philosophical Forum* 35:3 (September 2004).

Cavell, Stanley. "The availability of Wittgenstein's later philosophy." *The Philosophical Review* 71:1 (January 1962).

—. *The Claim of Reason: Wittgenstein, Skepticism, Morality and Tragedy.* Oxford: Oxford University Press, 1979.

—. "Declining decline." *This New Yet Unapproachable America: Lectures after Emerson after Wittgenstein.* Albuquerque: Living Batch Press, 1989, pp. 29–76.

—. "The argument of the ordinary: Scenes of instructions in Wittgenstein and in Kripke." *Conditions Handsome and Unhandsome: The Constitution of Emersonian Perfectionism.* Chicago: University of Chicago Press, 1990, 64–100.

—. "Notes and afterthoughts on the opening of Wittgenstein's *Investigations.*" *Philosophical Passages: Wittgenstein, Emerson, Austin, Derrida.* Oxford: Blackwell, 1995, pp. 125–86.

—. "Excursus on Wittgenstein's vision of language." In *The New Wittgenstein,* eds Alice Crary and Rupert Read. New York: Routledge, 2000, pp. 21–37.

Conant, James. "Must we show what we cannot say?" In *The Senses of Stanley Cavell,* eds R. Fleming and M. Payne. Lewisburg, PA: Bucknell University Press, 1989, pp. 242–83.

—. "Wittgenstein on meaning and use." *Philosophical Investigations* 21:3 (July 1998).

—. "On going the bloody *hard way* in philosophy." In *The Possibilities of Sense,* ed. John H. Whittaker. New York: Palgrave, 2002, pp. 85–129.

—. "What 'ethics' in the *Tractatus* is *not.*" In *Religion and Wittgenstein's Legacy,* eds D. Z. Phillips and M. Von der Ruhr. Burlington: Ashgate, 2005, pp. 39–88.

Crary, Alice. "Wittgenstein's philosophy in relation to political thought." In *The New Wittgenstein,* eds Alice Crary and Rupert Read. New York: Routledge, 2000, pp. 118–45.

Davis, John B. "Gramsci, Sraffa, Wittgenstein: Philosophical linkages." *European Journal of Economic Thought* 9:3 (Autumn 2002).

Deleuze, Gilles. *Essays Critical and Clinical.* Trans. Daniel W. Smith and Michael A. Greco. Minneapolis: University of Minnesota Press, 1997.

—. "Immanence: A life." *Pure Immanence: Essays on A Life.* Trans. Anne Boyman. New York: Zone Books, 2001, pp. 25–33.

Derrida, Jacques. *Learning to Live Finally: The Last Interview.* Trans. P. A. Brault and M. Naas. Hoboken, NJ: Melville, 2007.

Diamond, Cora. *The Realistic Spirit: Wittgenstein, Philosophy, and the Mind.* Cambridge, MA: MIT Press, 1991.

—. "Rules: Looking in the right place." In *Wittgenstein: Attention to Particulars*, eds D. Z. Phillips and Peter Winch. New York: St. Martin's Press, 1998, pp. 12–34.

—. "Ethics, imagination, and the method of Wittgenstein's *Tractatus*." In *The New Wittgenstein*, eds Alice Crary and Rupert Read. New York: Routledge, 2000, pp. 149–73.

—. "Criss-cross philosophy." In *Wittgenstein at Work: Method in the Philosophical Investigations*, eds Erich Ammereller and Eugen Fischer. New York: Routledge, 2004, pp. 201–20.

Drury, Maurice O'C. "Some notes on conversations with Wittgenstein" and "Conversation with Wittgenstein." In *Ludwig Wittgenstein, Personal Recollections*, ed. R. Rhees. Oxford: Blackwell, 1981, pp. 91–181.

Emmett, Kathleen. "Forms of life." *Philosophical Investigations* 13:3 (July 1990).

Foucault, Michel. *Discipline and Punish: The Birth of the Prison*. Trans. Alan Sheridan. New York: Vintage Books, 1979.

Frege, Gottlob. *Foundations of Arithmetic*. Trans. J. L. Austin. Evanston: Northwestern University Press, 1980.

Friedlander, Eli. *Signs of Sense: Reading Wittgenstein's Tractatus*. Cambridge, MA: Harvard University Press, 2001.

Garver, Newton. *This Complicated Form of Life: Essays on Wittgenstein*. Chicago: Open Court, 1994.

Goethe, Johann Wolfgang von. *Selected Verse*. Ed. David Luke. London: Penguin Books, 1964.

Heidegger, Martin. "On the essence of truth." In *Basic Writings*, ed. David Farrell Krell. New York: Harper Collins, 1993, pp. 111–38.

—. *Being and Time*. Trans. Joan Stambaugh. Albany: State University of New York Press, 1996.

Hilmy, Stephen. "Wittgensteinian relativism and the dynamic view of language." *The Later Wittgenstein: The Emergence of a New Philosophical Method*. Oxford: Blackwell, 1987, pp. 138–89.

Hinman, Lawrence M. "Can a form of life be wrong?" *Philosophy: The Journal of the Royal Institute of Philosophy* 58 (July 1983).

Kripke, Saul. *Wittgenstein on Rules and Private Language*. Cambridge, MA: Harvard University Press, 1982.

Lear, Jonathan. "Leaving the world alone." *The Journal of Philosophy* 91 (1982).

Lurie, Yuval. "Culture as a human form of life." *International Philosophical Quarterly* 32:2 (June 1992).

—. *Tracking the Meaning of life: A Philosophical Journey*. Columbia, MO: University of Missouri Press, 2006.

Mach, Ernst. *The Analysis of Sensations*. Trans. C. M. Williams. London: Routledge, 1996.

Magnanini, Dina. "Tolstoy and Wittgenstein as imitators of Christ." In *Wittgenstein and His Impact on Contemporary Thought, Vol. 2*, eds. E. Leinfellner, W. Leifellner, H. Berghel, and A. Hübner. Vienna: Holder-Pichler-Tempsky, 1978, pp. 490–3.

Malcolm, Norman. "Wittgenstein's *Philosophical Investigations*." *The Philosophical Review* 63:4 (October 1954).

—. *Ludwig Wittgenstein: A Memoir*. Oxford: Oxford University Press, 1970.

—. *Thought and Knowledge*. Ithaca, NY: Cornell University Press, 1977.

—. *Wittgenstein: A Religious Point of View?* Ed. Peter Winch. Ithaca, NY: Cornell University Press, 1994.

Melville, Herman. "Bartleby the scrivener: A story of Wall Street." *Great Short Works of Herman Melville*. New York: Harper Perennial, 2004, pp. 39–74.

Monk, Ray. *Ludwig Wittgenstein: The Duty of Genius*. New York: Penguin, 1990.

Moore, G. E. "Proof of the external world." *Philosophical Papers*. London: George Allen, 1959, pp. 127–50.

Mulhall, Stephen. *Wittgenstein's Private Language: Grammar, Nonesense, and Imagination in Philosophical Investigations §§243–315*. Oxford: Clarendon Press, 2007.

Nedo, Michael and Ranchetti, Michele. *Ludwig Wittgenstein: sein Leben in Bildern und Texten*. Frankfurt am Main : Suhrkamp, 1983.

Nietzsche, Friedrich. "On the uses and disadvantages of history for life." In *Untimely Meditations*. Ed. Daniel Breazeale, trans. R. J. Hollingdale. Cambridge: Cambridge University Press, 1997, pp. 57–124.

—. *The Genealogy of Morals*. Trans. Horace B. Samuel. Mineola, NY: Dover Publications, 2003.

Nyíri, J. C. "Wittgenstein's later work in relation to conservatism." In *Wittgenstein and His Times*, ed. Brian McGuinness. Oxford: Blackwell, 1982, pp. 44–68.

Pessoa, Fernando. *The Book of Disquiet*. Trans. Alfred M. Adam. New York: Pantheon, 1991.

Plato. *Phaedo*. Trans. R. Hackforth. Cambridge: Cambridge University Press, 1955.

Poe, Edgar Allen. "The premature burial." *Complete Stories and Poems of Edgar Allen Poe*. Garden City, NY: Doubleday, 1984, pp. 261–70.

Read, Rupert. "Wittgenstein and Marx on philosophical language." *Essays in Philosophy* 1:2 (June 2000).

Read, Rupert and Guetti, James. "Meaningful consequences." *Philosophical Forum* 30:4 (December 1999).

Rhees, Rush. *Discussions of Wittgenstein*. New York: Schocken Books, 1970.

Robinson, Christopher. "Why Wittgenstein is not conservative: Conventions and critique." *Theory and Event* 9:3 (2006).

Rorty, Richard. *Contingency, Irony, and Solidarity*. New York: Cambridge University Press, 1989.

Rudder-Baker, Lynne. "On the very idea of a form of life." *Inquiry: An Interdisciplinary Journal of Philosophy* 27 (July 1984).

Russell, Bertrand. "What is logic?" *The Collected Papers of Bertrand Russell, Vol. 6*. London: Routledge, 1992, pp. 54–6.

Scheman, Naomi. "Forms of life: Mapping the rough ground." In *The Cambridge Companion to Wittgenstein*, eds Hans D. Sluga and David G. Stern. New York: Cambridge University Press, 1996, pp. 383–410.

Schmitt, Carl. *Political Theology: Four Chapters on the Concept of Sovereignty*. Trans. George Schwab. Chicago: The University of Chicago Press, 2005.

Scholem, Gershom. Ed. *The Correspondence of Walter Benjamin and Gershom Scholem, 1932–1940*. Trans. Gary Smith and Andre Lefevere. Cambridge, MA: Harvard University Press, 1992.

—. *Walter Benjamin: The Story of a Friendship.* Trans. Harry Zohn. New York: New York Review of Books, 2001.

Sherry, Patrick. "Is religion a form of life?" *American Philosophical Quarterly* 9:2 (1972).

Spinoza, Baruch. *The Ethics; Treatise on the Emendation of the Intellect; Selected Letters.* Trans. Samuel Shirley. Indianapolis: Hackett Publishing, 1991.

Thompson, Caleb. "Wittgenstein, Tolstoy and the meaning of life." *Philosophical Investigations* 20:2 (April 1997).

—. "Wittgenstein's confessions." *Philosophical Investigations* 23:1 (January 2000).

—. "Wittgenstein, Augustine, and the fantasy of ascent." *Philosophical Investigations* 25:2 (April 2002).

Thompson, Michael. "The representation of life." In *Virtues and Reasons: Philippa Foot and Moral Theory,* eds. R. Hursthouse, G. Lawrence, and W. Quinn. New York: Oxford University Press, 1995, pp. 247–96.

—. "Apprehending human form." In *Modern Moral Philosophy,* ed. Anthony O'Hear. New York: Cambridge University Press, 2004, pp. 47–74.

Tolstoy, Leo. *A Confession.* Trans. David Patterson. New York: Norton, 1983.

—. *Gospel in Brief.* Trans. Isabel Hapgood. Lincoln: University of Nebraska Press, 1997.

Warburg, Aby. *Der Bilderatlas Mnemosyne.* Berlin: Akademie Verlag, 2000.

Wertz, Spenser K. "On the philosophical genesis of the term form of life." *Southwest Philosophical Studies* VI: 2 (April 1981).

Whittaker, John H. "Language games and forms of life unconfused." *Philosophical Investigations* 1 (Fall 1978).

Winch, Peter. "The unity of Wittgenstein's philosophy." In *Studies in the Philosophy of Wittgenstein,* ed. Peter Winch. London: Kegan and Paul, 1969, pp. 1–19.

—. *The Idea of a Social Science.* London: Routledge, 1990.

Woolf, Virginia. *Mrs. Dalloway.* San Diego: Harcourt Brace, 1990.

Wright, Georg Henrik von. *Wittgenstein.* Minneapolis: University of Minnesota Press, 1982.

Index

Printed in Great Britain
by Amazon